THE HISTORY OF
MEDICINE

THE HISTORY OF
MEDICINE

HEALTHCARE AROUND THE WORLD
AND THROUGH THE AGES

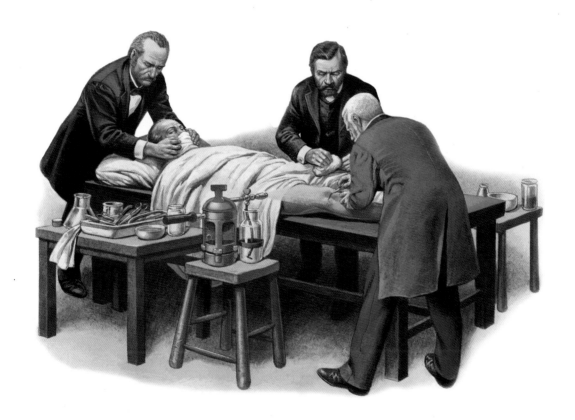

BRIAN WARD

ARMADILLO

This edition is published by Armadillo, an imprint of Anness Publishing Ltd, 108 Great Russell Street, London WC1B 3NA; info@anness.com

www.armadillobooks.co.uk; www.annesspublishing.com; twitter: @Anness_Books

Anness Publishing has a new picture agency outlet for images for publishing, promotions or advertising. Please visit our website www.practicalpictures.com for more information.

© Anness Publishing Ltd 2016

A CIP catalogue record for this book is available from the British Library.

Publisher: Joanna Lorenz
Produced by Miles Kelly Publishing Limited
Project Editor: Clare Oliver
Design: Sally Boothroyd

The publishers would like to thank the following artists who have contributed to this book:
Vanessa Card; Terry Gabbey (AFA); Sally Holmes; Richard Hook (Linden Artists); John James (Temple Rogers); Shane Marsh (LindenArtists); Peter Sarson; Rob Sheffield; Guy Smith (Mainline Design); Mike White (Temple Rogers); Janos Marffy; Roger Gorringe (Illustration Ltd.); Ch'en Ling; Terry Riley Studio; Peter Gregory; Mike Saunders; Helen Parsley (JM & A Associates); Alison Winfield; Andy Beckett (Illustration Ltd.); Clive Spong (Linden Artists).
Maps: Steve Sweet & Stuart Squires (SGA).

The publishers wish to thank the following for supplying photographs for this book: Page 9 (TL) Mary Evans Picture Library; 10 (BR) Mary Evans Picture Library; 11 (BC) Buddy Mays/ CORBIS; 22 (BC) Mary Evans Picture Library; 23 (TL) Mary Evans Picture Library; 24 (CR) Ann Ronan Picture Library; 25 (TR) Bettmann/ CORBIS; 27 (TR) The Bridgeman Art Library, (CL) Bettmann/ CORBIS; 30 (CR) Bettmann/ CORBIS; 31 (BL) CORBIS; 34 (BL) Mary Evans Picture Library; 36 (TL) Mary Evans Picture Library; 37 (BL) Hulton-Deutsch Collection/ CORBIS; 38 (C) Bettmann/ CORBIS; 40 (TL) CORBIS (BL) Hulton-Deutsch Collection/ CORBIS; 41 (TR) CORBIS; 42 (CR) Bettmann/ CORBIS; 43 (TR) Bettmann/ CORBIS; 45 (BL) CORBIS, (BC) Bettmann/ CORBIS; 46 (BC) Ann Ronan Picture Library; 47 (TL) Nathan Benn/ CORBIS; 48 (BL) Bettmann/ CORBIS; 49 (TR) Bettmann/ CORBIS; 51 (TR) Mary Evans Picture Library; 53 (CR) Lisa M McGeady/ CORBIS, (C) Lynda Richardson, (BL) photo courtesy of the British School of Shiatsu-Do (London); 55 (CR) AFP/ CORBIS; 57 (BL) Roger Ressmeyer/ CORBIS; 58 (TR) Ann Ronan Picture Library, (BL) CORBIS; 60 (C) Hank Morgan/ Science Photo Library.
All other pictures from
Dover Publications and Miles Kelly archives.

Manufacturer: Anness Publishing Ltd,
108 Great Russell Street, London WC1B 3NA, England
For Product Tracking go to: www.annesspublishing.com/tracking
Batch: 7566-23833-1127

CONTENTS

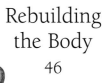

Introduction

What is medicine? And what is health? In different cultures and at different times you would have received widely varying answers to these questions. In the modern Western medical tradition, the main objective is to get rid of disease, and then to keep people healthy. In earlier times, Western medicine depended on a muddled mixture of prayer, folk remedies and theories going back to the Arab civilizations and beyond that to the ancient Greeks. True advances in medical care did not take place until the 19th century, and it was not until the 20th century that medicine was able to reduce the high death rates caused by infections. Eastern medicine took a different line, which was that the whole body had to be treated in order to keep it healthy and to prevent disease from appearing. Now, in the 21st century, Western medicine has begun to accept the idea of keeping the whole body healthy.

Disease is when the normal body does not function properly, but it is more difficult to define health. A person aged 70 or more may feel that they are in perfect health, but a younger person would not be happy to experience the aches, pains and breathlessness that often accompany ageing. So health needs to be considered in terms of our

▲ TRADITIONAL MEDICINES
Chinese medicine developed from a totally different background to science-based Western medicine. It treats the whole body by restoring the balance of forces flowing within it. There is growing interest in this and other forms of traditional medicine.

▼ KEY DATES
The panel charts the history of medicine, from the earliest uses of herbs and magic as cures, to the invention of state-of-the-art technologies.

▼ CAUTERIZING IRON
Medical techniques become out-dated as better knowledge and technology lead to an improved way of doing things. For centuries, a red-hot iron was used to seal or cauterize the blood vessels and prevent bleeding after surgery. This agonizing process usually led to infection. Today, high-tech laser beams seal a wound safely and painlessly.

ANCIENT TIMES

15,000BC Cave paintings in France show shamanic rituals.

2700BC Legendary Shen Nong discovers herbalism.

2600BC Imhotep describes ancient Egyptian medicine.

*c.***2000BC** Legendary date for the writing of the *Nei Ching*.

*c.***1700BC** Code of Hammurabi lays down laws for doctors.

Hammurabi, king of Babylon

1550BC Ebers papyrus records Egyptian medical practices.

1200BC Asclepius sets up healing places in ancient Greece.

460BC Birth of Hippocrates, who founds Greek medicine.

Hippocrates

*c.***300BC** The medical school and library at Alexandria is founded.

AD40–*c.***90** Dioscorides writes manual of herbal medicine.

AD129-216 Galen enlarges on earlier Greek writings and begins experimental medical studies.

THE MIDDLE AGES

AD832 Non-Islamic medical texts are translated in Baghdad.

*c.***AD800** Rhazes prepares his medical compendium.

*c.***AD1000** Avicenna produces the *Canon of Medicine*.

1100–1300 Medical schools are founded throughout Europe.

1215 The Pope decrees that all doctors need Church approval.

*c.***1200–1300** Professional medical organizations are set up.

1258 Medical texts preserved by the Arabs flow back to the West.

Paracelsus

THE RENAISSANCE

1527 Paracelsus lays the ground for studies into chemical treatment of diseases.

1543 Vesalius publishes accurate illustrations of human anatomy.

1628 William Harvey publishes his theory of blood circulation.

1665 King Charles II and the royal court flee London during the Great Plague.

expectations for normal life. Even ageing itself is thought of almost as a disease in some Western cultures, where people are living longer. Thanks to modern medicine, today people can live an active life into extreme old age, while in earlier times they might have been crippled by heart disease or arthritis. However, in some developing countries where malnutrition and infection are common, 40 years is still considered to be a good life expectancy.

Killer diseases, that used to wipe out as many as half of the children in a family, have been brought under control by drugs and vaccination in Western countries. However, nature still has a few surprises for modern medicine. New diseases such as AIDS have appeared and these are not yet under control. Some of the old, familiar microbes have found ways to beat modern antibiotics and are threatening health once more. The only real conquest of disease has been the eradication of smallpox. There are a few more diseases, such as polio, measles and leprosy, that might be conquered soon.

Medicine has made other huge advances. Doctors have the technology with which to examine almost every part of the body. Scientists are beginning to understand the complex chemical reactions that power the body. Surgery, which has been performed for thousands of years, has made great leaps with the techniques for transplantation of body organs and artificial organs. One thing is certain – no one can be sure what advances medicine will make in the future.

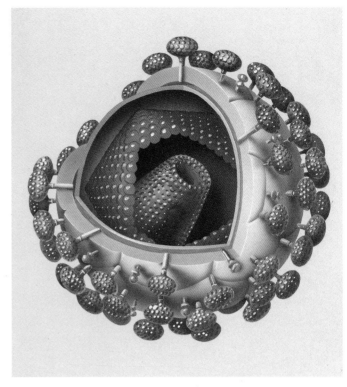

▲ HIV VIRUS
Recent understanding of the structure of viruses, such as HIV, has revealed how they overcome the body's natural immune system. Research into viruses can reveal their weak points, so that effective drugs can be designed to attack them.

MODERN TIMES

1673 Van Leeuwenhoek makes the first microscope and discovers microbes.

1714 Gabriel Fahrenheit invents the mercury thermometer.

1796 Edward Jenner vaccinates against smallpox using cowpox.

1819 René Laënnec introduces the first stethoscope.

Laënnec's stethoscope

1847 Ignaz Semmelweiss demonstrates that infection is spread by unwashed hands.

1853 Queen Victoria uses chloroform as an anaesthetic during childbirth.

chloroform mask

1854 John Snow demonstrates that cholera is spread through contaminated drinking water.

1865 Joseph Lister carries out the first operation using carbolic acid as an antiseptic.

1878 Louis Pasteur presents his case for the germ theory of infection.

1882 Robert Koch discovers the tubercle bacillus that causes TB.

1885 Louis Pasteur successfully tests his rabies vaccine.

1895 X-rays are discovered by Wilhelm Röntgen.

1898 Marie Curie discovers the radioactive element radium.

1901–2 Blood groups are described by Karl Landsteiner, making transfusion practical.

1902 Frederick Treves makes removal of the appendix a popular treatment for appendicitis.

Marie Curie

1928 Alexander Fleming discovers penicillin.

1953 James Watson and Francis Crick discover the structure of DNA.

1954 The first successful kidney transplant is performed.

DNA

1955 Jonas Salk introduces the first polio vaccine.

1961 Thalidomide (a sedative) is withdrawn after causing birth defects.

1967 Christiaan Barnard carries out the first human heart transplant.

1974 The last natural case of smallpox occurs.

1983 HIV is identified.

2001 The Lindbergh Operation, the first remotely controlled surgery.

Earliest Medicine

EARLY PEOPLE'S REMAINS contain evidence of attempts at medical care. The most striking of these are skulls with neatly drilled or cut holes. The process of making these holes is called trepanning. The holes may have been made to allow a disease to escape from the body. Trepanned skulls have been found in Europe and in South America. Remarkably, some of them show signs that the cut edges of bone had healed, so the patient had survived for some time after the operation. Some even show evidence of being trepanned on several different occasions.

Herbal medicine was probably also administered from the earliest times. It can still be seen in the great apes, such as chimpanzees. Chimps sometimes chew herbs that are not part of their normal diet, probably for their medicinal effects. The remains of herbs are not uncommon in ancient burials, and have also been found in association with the burials of Neanderthals,

▲ TREPANNING TOOLS
Stone Age people used a drill to cut a hole in the skull. This was a wooden stick with a sharpened piece of flint at the tip. Flints were later used with a bow drill. Sometimes the drill was tipped with volcanic glass or even a shark's tooth.

who were ancient relatives of modern people.

Although prehistoric people must have suffered from many diseases, they probably did not experience the rapidly spreading infections that later caused epidemics. They lived in small groups, so there were not enough people for diseases to spread quickly.

By 3000BC people were beginning to live in huge cities, such as Babylon. Epidemic diseases appeared, many of which are recorded in ancient documents. By about 1700BC Babylonian doctors had to follow a number of laws. These were written down in the Code of Hammurabi. One practice was to sacrifice animals and look at their organs to foretell if the patient would die.

The ancient Egyptians left careful records that describe a whole range of medical

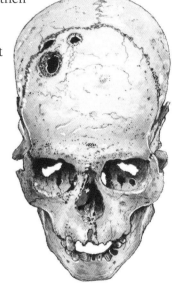

▶ HOLES IN THE HEAD
This skull was found in Jericho and dates to 2000BC. It has three carefully cut trepanning holes, together with a healed hole. The holes are round, which tells us that they must have been drilled into the skull. In other skull finds, there are square holes, that were cut out with a knife.

MESOPOTAMIA AND EGYPT
The oldest surviving medical text is the Ebers papyrus from Egypt. It dates back to about 1550BC. This papyrus scroll is more than 20m/65ft long and describes many diseases and remedies. It includes over 700 drugs and 800 medicine recipes. There is even a cure for crocodile bites. The Ebers papyrus has instructions for mixing up these medicines into ointments, poultices (compresses), pills and inhalations. There are also descriptions of protective amulets (charms) and spells. Many of the medicines would have had little effect, but some were drugs still familiar today, including opium and cannabis.

▼ THE FIRST DOCTOR
Imhotep was an ancient Egyptian scribe and priest who lived 4,500 years ago. He left many detailed descriptions of diseases and treatments. After his death, he was made into a god.

◀ SURGICAL TOOLS
These bronze and copper knives are from ancient Mesopotamia. They may have been used to remove organs from dead bodies.

▶ CODE OF CONDUCT
Hammurabi, king of Babylon, laid down 17 rules for doctors in the Code of Hammurabi, his collection of all Babylonian laws. The rules included guidelines on punishments for doctors if their treatment did not work.

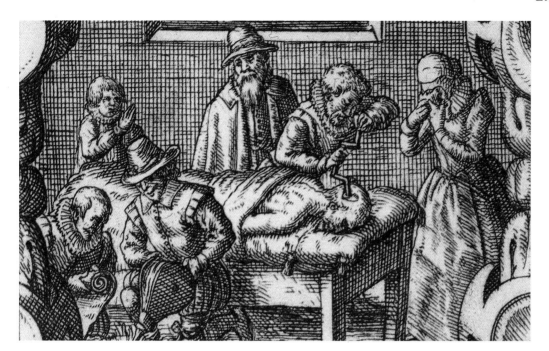

◀ TREPANNING IN PROGRESS
This picture from the 1500s shows a doctor trepanning his patient. In the ancient world, trepanning was often carried out to release spirits from the brain. Trepanning is extremely dangerous because it allows bacteria to come into contact with the brain surface. Many patients must have died.

▼ MEDICINE IN THE WILD
Animals such as this baby gorilla search out medicinal herbs in order to treat their ailments. Even carnivores, such as cats, sometimes chew leaves and stems. This may be a way to obtain extra nutrients.

procedures and drugs. Egyptian doctors began to specialize in treating particular organs or diseases. The most famous was Imhotep, who was also a high priest, an architect and an astrologer. The Egyptians believed that spirits crept into the body and caused disease. They used surgery to set broken bones and sew up wounds. However, they took little interest in internal anatomy (the inside workings of the human body). This is surprising, as they must have learned about it through their interest in mummifying (preserving) the bodies of the dead. Most Egyptian medicine consisted of herbal treatments.

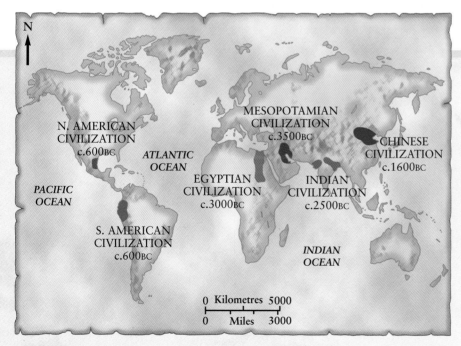

▲ EARLIEST MEDICINE
Finds or written records provide evidence of medicine used by the civilizations shown here, but it is almost certain that medicine was known in all ancient cultures.

N. AMERICAN CIVILIZATION c.600BC

ATLANTIC OCEAN

PACIFIC OCEAN

S. AMERICAN CIVILIZATION c.600BC

MESOPOTAMIAN CIVILIZATION c.3500BC

EGYPTIAN CIVILIZATION c.3000BC

INDIAN CIVILIZATION c.2500BC

CHINESE CIVILIZATION c.1600BC

INDIAN OCEAN

0 Kilometres 5000
0 Miles 3000

Key Dates

- 10,000–2000BC Evidence of ancient Egyptian medical practice.

- 5000BC Trepanned skull at Ensisheim, France, is the oldest evidence we have of trepanning.

- c.2686–2613BC Life of the Egyptian doctor, Imhotep.

- 1792–1750BC Hammurabi rules in Babylon.

- 1550BC The Ebers papyrus is written in Egypt.

- 650BC Mesopotamian clay tablets describe herbal cures and accurately describe a *migtu* (epileptic seizure).

Shamans and the Supernatural

A
S ISOLATED COMMUNITIES
developed, so did the idea
of an individual who could
combine the function of healer with
the ability to speak to the gods and
spirits. In some early French cave
paintings, made about 17,000 years
ago, there are pictures of men in
animal masks performing
ritual dances. These are
what we call shamans,
and they still exist
in many cultures around
the world. Shamans
are found in Arctic
regions and especially
in Siberia, among some
Native North Americans
and South Americans, in
Southeast Asia and in the
Pacific Islands. In West Africa, shamans are often
known as medicine men or witch doctors. Their
activities include medical treatment with drugs and
prayer, and sometimes the laying of curses on an
enemy. People believe that shamans also have the
power to cause illness, to ensure fertility or the birth
of male children, and to prevent disease by the use of
ointments, talismans (charms) and fetishes (magical
objects). Shamans are thought to talk with gods, spirits

▲ ASHANTI DOLL
*Shamans heal by
magic. They often
use dolls to represent
their patients, or to
represent the spirits
that will aid in the
healing ceremony.*

▶ SHAMAN HEALING
CEREMONY
*During the healing ritual,
such as this ceremony in
Cameroon, West Africa, the
shaman dances around the
patient and chants prayers
to the spirits.*

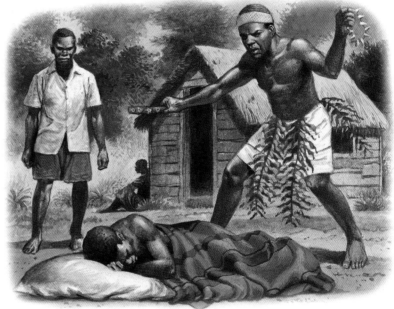

NATIVE AMERICAN MEDICINE
All the Native American tribes had
shamans. Those of the Ojibwa tribe
formed secret societies and even
specialized in particular types of medicine,
such as herbalism. Disease was often seen
as punishment for behaving badly or not
worshipping the spirits properly. The
Navajo cure was to appeal to the spirits
by means of songs, dance, prayer,
sweat baths, massage and
making sand paintings. Bull-
roarers were flat pieces of wood,
tied to cord that made a roaring
sound when whirled around at
high speed. They were used to
invoke (call up) wind or rain
and drive out evil spirits.

▶ MEDICINE MAN
There were over 300 different
tribes of Native Americans and
they all had different ways of life
and traditions. This medicine
man is from the Blackfoot tribe,
who lived on the plains of the
northwestern USA in what is
now the state of Montana.

◀ MAGIC
NECKLACE
This magical
amulet was worn
by an Apache
medicine man. It is
made from glass
beads and human
teeth, some of which
are still embedded in
part of the jawbone.

and the dead. They often ask the spirits for things, such as a good harvest, or victory in battle over other villages or tribes.

The shaman usually acts as a local religious leader. Shamanism is not organized like the major world religions. It is a collection of a whole range of folk beliefs and myths. The shaman is able to leave his body and enter a trance, where he does not appear to be aware of what is going on around him. He does this through the use of drugs, dancing, music or, sometimes, an epileptic fit.

In most cultures where shamans exist, illness is blamed on the soul leaving the body. In a trance, the shaman finds the soul, which may have been stolen by witchcraft or magic, and persuades it to return to the body. This is a long process, often made dangerous by the use of drugs. If the patient dies, the shaman has to make a treacherous voyage to take the soul of the dead person safely to its new home.

Sometimes an illness is blamed on an object that has been put inside the sick person by magic. In these cases the shaman sucks hard at the affected area, then spits out pieces of wood or stone. These are said to be the cause of the problem. Shamans use various types of instruments and charms for their cures, such as hollow bones to suck out poison, sharp flints for cutting the skin and causing bleeding and, often, masks and other ritual clothing.

◀ BAHUNGANA FETISH
A fetish is an object believed to possess magical powers. This one has a medicine bag like a shaman uses. It is covered with figures that help to give it its power.

▶ YOMBE FETISH
This fetish comes from the Yombe tribe of the Republic of Congo. It can be used to cure or curse, by driving nails into the image during a magical ritual. The nails are pushed into the part of the body that needs to be made better or harmed.

▼ SQUAWROOT
North American medicine men used the roots of the black cohosh, or squawroot, as a painkiller. It has now been adopted by Western herbalists.

▶ SAND PAINTING
Navajo Native Americans used grains of pigmented sand to create magical pictures called sand paintings. Some were big enough for the sick person to sit in the middle of them during the healing ceremony.

Key Dates

- 15,000BC French cave paintings show evidence of ritual dances.

- c.3000BC An amber horse from this date shows the use of amulets to ward off evil spirits and sickness.

- AD1492 Christopher Columbus 'discovers' the Americas.

- 1520s Cabeza de Vaca witnesses medicine men curing the sick by blowing on the patient.

- 1800s Tradition of medicine men disappears as European settlers destroy and fragment Native American tribes.

Ayurvedic Medicine

THE *VEDAS* are a series of Hindu texts written in India between 1200BC and 900BC, though they are probably based on much older stories. In among the religious parts of the *Vedas* are explanations of the workings of the body and detailed descriptions of diseases, including dropsy and cancers. Treatments recommended in the *Vedas* included herbal remedies and also prayers and magic rituals to expel demons. Vedic medicine was in use up to around 1000BC.

After 1000BC a new school of medicine emerged in India, still based on the *Vedas*, but drawing in beliefs from other systems, such as Buddhism. This is known as Ayurvedic (knowledge of life) medicine. Its principles were written down in two influential books. These were the *Caraka-samhita* and the *Sushruta-samhita*, written by two doctors called Caraka and Sushruta. Both believed that desires upset the body's balance so they have to be satisfied in moderation.

The Hindus believed that the body was built from three essences or elements. These were air or breath, phlegm and bile. They had to be in balance for a person to enjoy good health. The essences interacted to produce the body's flesh, fat, marrow, blood, bone, chyle (fatty fluid) and semen. Ayurvedic treatment involved restoring the balance of the essences, with a combination of prayer, herbal medicine, diet and, sometimes, surgery.

Indian doctors were very skilled in making a diagnosis (identifying a disease). As apprentices, they had to memorize passages from the *Vedas*. During the examination of the patient, appropriate verses would come to mind. The verses helped the doctor to

▲ FIRE AND FEVER
Agni was the Hindu god of fire. People prayed to him in cases of fever.

▶ LOTUS POSITION
Meditation (deep thought) and exercise are important parts of Indian medicine. The lotus position is one of the poses used in yoga during meditation. Performing yoga helps the body to reach a state of spiritual enlightenment and keeps the three essences in balance.

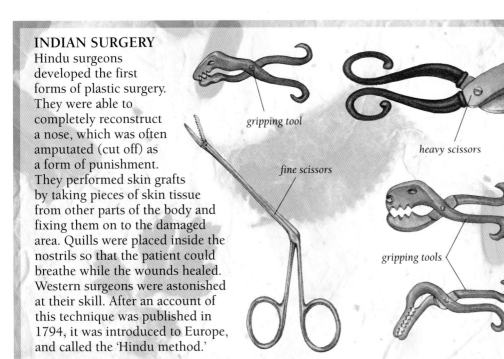

INDIAN SURGERY
Hindu surgeons developed the first forms of plastic surgery. They were able to completely reconstruct a nose, which was often amputated (cut off) as a form of punishment. They performed skin grafts by taking pieces of skin tissue from other parts of the body and fixing them on to the damaged area. Quills were placed inside the nostrils so that the patient could breathe while the wounds healed. Western surgeons were astonished at their skill. After an account of this technique was published in 1794, it was introduced to Europe, and called the 'Hindu method.'

gripping tool

fine scissors

heavy scissors

gripping tools

◀ SURGICAL TOOLS
Ayurvedic doctors developed some sophisticated surgical techniques. They used steel instruments, such as these, dating from about AD1100, to carry out their operations. Steel does not rust, which makes these instruments far more hygienic.

make a proper diagnosis and suggest the right treatment. There was a large range of herbal medicines to choose from, as well as drugs prepared from animal parts or minerals. Drugs used included the dung or urine of elephants, and the eggs of peacocks and crocodiles.

Partly for religious reasons, hygiene was very important to Ayurvedic surgeons. Doctors stressed the importance of washing the body and cleaning the teeth regularly.

Hindu surgeons were highly skilled. Operations included removing cancers and cataracts, repairing broken bones, stitching wounds, and performing caesarean births and amputations. They were even able to remove bladder stones. Thanks to their good hygiene, surgeons in India in 800BC had a higher survival rate among their patients than those in Europe up until the 1800s.

▲ LORD BRAHMA HOLDS COURT
Ayurvedic medicine was said to have been developed by Brahma, one of the Hindu trinity of ruling gods. The Vedas are a whole body of knowledge containing religious and philosophical teaching, as well as information on medicine.

▲ BODY PLAN
Ayurvedic medicine developed a plan of the inside workings of the body. It mapped a whole system of furnaces, tubes and valves. These had no basis in reality, because Hindus were forbidden by their religion to cut open a dead body.

▼ DR ANT
Wounds were 'stitched' by the use of fierce biting ants. The ants gripped the edges of the wound and held them tightly together.

▶ NOSE REBUILDING
Ayurvedic surgeons developed the techniques of plastic surgery. They knew that it was essential to keep a bridge of living tissue in the skin flap that they used to reconstruct a nose. This maintained the blood supply and prevented the grafted tissue from dying.

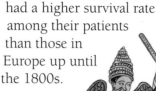

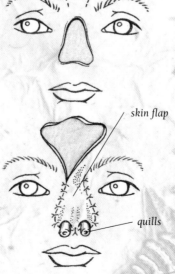

skin flap

skin flap

quills

Key Dates

- 1200–900BC The *Vedas* are written.

- 200BC First descriptions of yoga techniques are written down in the *Yoga-sutras*.

- AD100 Final version of the *Caraka-samhita* is written.

- AD600s Final version of the *Sushruta-samhita* is written.

- AD1000s Islamic invaders bring new medical practices to India.

- 1500s European settlers bring Western medical ideas to India.

- 1793 British doctors first observe Hindus performing reconstructive surgery.

Chinese Medicine

CHINESE MEDICINE developed over thousands of years, almost without any outside influences from other medical systems. The *Nei Ching* (Book of Medicine) is an ancient medical work. According to legend, it was written over 4,000 years ago by the Yellow Emperor, Huang Ti. The book was more likely to have been written some time about 200BC, but it has formed the basis for most Chinese medical literature since.

Chinese medicine is largely based on the concept of *yin* and *yang*, which stand for opposing states and conditions. *Yin* represents states such as feminine, dark and wet. *Yang* represents the opposing states of masculine, light and dry. In the *Nei Ching*, *yin* and *yang* are said to control the body, which is thought of as a tiny country with rulers and administrators. The 'country' also has a communication system of 12 rivers, based on the great rivers of China. These rivers divide into much smaller channels which carry blood and *ch'i* (vital energy).

These channels connect organs to one another. For example, the kidney connects to the ear, the lungs to the nose and the heart to the tongue. When these channels are in good working order, the body is healthy. Points along the channels can be used to influence the flow of *ch'i*.

As with Hinduism, Chinese religions discouraged dissection. For this reason, medicine was based largely

▲ YIN AND YANG
The symbol for yin *and* yang *represents the rule of opposites that is so important in Chinese medicine.* Yin *is the force that represents qualities such as darkness. Its opposite,* yang, *stands for qualities such as light. Chinese medicine attempts to restore the balance between these opposites.*

▶ HUANG TI
The Yellow Emperor, Huang Ti, lived from 2698BC to 2598BC. He was said to be the author of the great Chinese medical work called the Nei Ching. *This forms the basis of all Chinese medicine.*

RESTORING THE BALANCE

The Chinese doctor was only paid as long as his patient remained healthy. So if a patient became ill, it was very important to restore the balance of *ch'i* and other elements within the body. This was done with a mixture of exercise, contemplation (thought or meditation), diet and other means. Many Chinese drugs were made from ingredients that were believed to have special effects. For example, organs from a tiger were thought to pass on some of that animal's power.

▶ DOCTOR AND PATIENT
Traditional Chinese medicine involves long discussion between the doctor and patient. The doctor treats the whole body, not just a small diseased part.

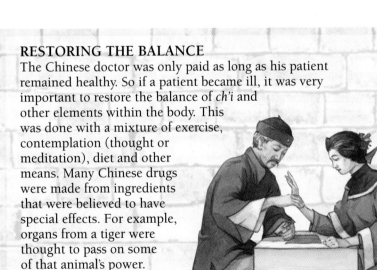

◀ MAMMOTH TEETH
So-called dragon teeth are still ground up and widely used in Chinese medicine. Of course, there are no such creatures as dragons. Huge teeth taken from the dug-up remains of ancient mammoths are often used by pharmacists, but so are the teeth of many other extinct animals, including those of the huge ape, *Gigantopithecus*.

▼ GINSENG
This root contains many substances which have powerful effects on the body. Extracts are widely used as a stimulant or tonic. The ginseng root may have appealed to early Chinese pharmacists because it looked a bit like a human body.

◀ PAGE FROM THE NEI CHING
The Nei Ching *explains how the forces* yin *and* yang *interact and affect the flow of* ch'i. *According to the* Nei Ching, *the human body, like all other matter, is made of five basic elements – fire, earth, water, metal and wood.*

▶ SHEN NONG
This legendary emperor lived in about 2700BC and is said to have discovered Chinese herbal medicine. He described 365 different medical plants. His teachings were written down about 2,000 years ago in a book called the Bencao Jing.

on these channels and their influences on the body. Treatments often involved the use of acupuncture, where needles were inserted into one of the hundreds of points where *ch'i* channels were thought to run. This stimulated (perked up) the flow of *ch'i* and restored good health. Sometimes cones of dried herbs were burned on the skin at these points, for the same purpose. Acupuncture has been used for more than 4,500 years. It remains central to Chinese medicine and is also used in the West, especially as a treatment for pain and a cure for addiction (dependency on a drug).

Chinese medicine depends mostly on herbal remedies. Many of these herbs have been incorporated into Western medicine, such as castor oil, camphor, chaulmoogra oil to treat leprosy and iron to treat anaemia. Ginseng is a widely-known Chinese stimulant, used to keep a person alert.

The ancient Chinese invented vaccination as a way to treat smallpox. They injected a small amount of pus from a smallpox sore into healthy people. This gave them a mild form of the disease and made them immune (resistant) to full-blown infection. Europeans did not discover vaccination until the AD1700s.

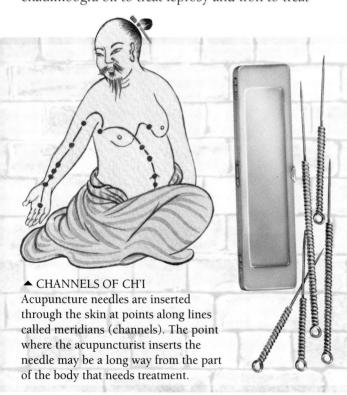

▲ CHANNELS OF CH'I
Acupuncture needles are inserted through the skin at points along lines called meridians (channels). The point where the acupuncturist inserts the needle may be a long way from the part of the body that needs treatment.

◀ ACUPUNCTURE NEEDLES
Acupuncturists (people who carry out acupuncture) use very long needles. They may be inserted as deeply as 25cm/10in into the body. Then the needles are wiggled or twirled to restore the flow of *ch'i*. Modern acupuncturists often pass a small electrical current through the needle.

Key Dates

- 2700sBC Life of legendary emperor Shen Nong, who discovered herbal medicine.

- 2698–2598BC The reign of Huang Ti, legendary founder of Chinese medicine.

- 200sBC The *Nei Ching* is written.

- AD280 Wang Shu-ho writes his 12-volume *Mei Ching* (Book of the Pulse).

- 1601 Yang Chi-chou writes his ten-volume *Ch'en-Chiu Ta-Ch'eng*, describing acupuncture.

- 1600s The first descriptions of Chinese medical practice reach the West.

Hippocrates and the Greeks

▲ SERPENT AND STAFF
A snake coiled around a wooden staff was the symbol of the Greek physician Asclepius, who lived around 1200BC. Even today, it is still used as a sign for the medical profession in many countries around the world.

THE ANCIENT GREEK DOCTOR Asclepius lived in about 1200BC. According to legend, he was so successful in curing disease that he became a god. The sick went and slept in his temples, known as *asklepia*. They believed that Asclepius would cure them in the night. Diet and mineral baths were part of the cure but treatment of disease was almost entirely a matter for prayer and magical rituals. However, from about 400BC Greek philosophers began to look for a more practical approach to disease.

The ancient Greeks had a great deal of contact with the Middle East and Asia, due to the conquests of Alexander the Great. In India they may have come across Vedic beliefs. This could explain how Greek philosophers came to believe that the universe was made up of four elements – air, earth, fire and water. This led to the idea

▲ THE FOUR HUMOURS
This medieval illustration shows the four humours. Greek philosophers held that the body was made up of these four elements – blood, phlegm, yellow bile or choler, and black bile or melancholy. These had to be kept in balance.

TREATING DISEASE
Hippocrates and his fellow doctors believed their job was to help the body to heal itself. Drugs were seldom used, although opium was used to relieve pain. Surgery was understood but was not very common. The Greeks have left behind detailed descriptions of trepanning, even advising surgeons to dip the knife or drill into cold water every now and then so it did not become too hot from rubbing against the bone. The writings of Hippocrates include a method for treating a dislocated (out of joint) shoulder that is still in use today. It is called the Hippocratic method.

▶ MANDRAKE
The root of the mandrake plant was believed to be a powerful magical charm because it looked rather like a human body. Mandrake is actually very poisonous.

▼ DOCTOR ON THE GO
Greek doctors moved around to meet their patients, on trips called *epidemics*. They were skilled in examining patients and accurate in diagnosing diseases, but they had only limited treatments available.

▲ BLOODLETTING
A Greek vase, made in about 470BC, shows a doctor preparing to bleed a patient by opening a vein. The blood would have been collected in the jar hanging on the wall behind them.

◄ FATHER OF MEDICINE
Hippocrates was the greatest of the ancient Greek doctors, and his influence persists to this day. He is said to have written more than 70 books on medicine and surgery. The Hippocratic Oath (promise) outlined the responsibilites that Hippocrates believed doctors had to their patients and to society. Doctors still try to live up to these today.

▶ VOTIVE TABLET
It was common to dedicate a tablet to the gods in thanks for a cure. This votive tablet is dedicated to Asclepius, probably in thanks for treatment of varicose veins, which can be seen on the leg that Asclepius is holding.

that the body was made up of four humours, or elements, too.

This belief was held by Hippocrates, the father of Western medicine. He was born in Kos around 460BC. Little is known about him. Even his surviving medical works were actually written by other people. Hippocrates said that diseases had natural causes. He stressed the importance of diagnosis and encouraged doctors to write down all they could about how a disease developed. He thought the body would heal itself and that this process could be sped up through diet, exercise and rest. These helped to restore the balance of the humours. If the disease did not respond, humours were removed by bloodletting (removing blood), or by making the patient sweat. These treatments often worked, even though the reasoning behind them was wrong. This is probably why the theory of humours survived into the 1800s in Western medicine, and so did Hippocratic treatments.

▶ SPREAD OF GREEK MEDICINE
Ancient Greek ideas spread around the Mediterranean, and through the Middle East and Egypt. In turn, herbal remedies and treatments from these areas were incorporated into Greek medicine. Later, after some initial resistance, the Romans also adopted Greek methods of medicine and surgery.

Key Dates

- 1200BC Asclepius sets up healing places. He is later worshipped as a god.

- 490–430BC Life of Empedocles, who described the four humours.

- 460–377BC Life of Hippocrates.

- 429BC An important medical school is founded at Cyrene.

- 356–323BC Life of Alexander the Great, whose empire stretched as far as India.

- c.300BC The famous medical school is founded at Alexandria.

- c.100BC Greek doctors take their knowledge to Rome.

Roman Medicine

▲ CELSUS
In around 25BC, the Roman nobleman Celsus wrote his huge encyclopedia. One of its volumes, De medicina, recorded all that was known about Greek and Roman medicine.

THE FAMOUS GREEK school at Alexandria remained the hub of medical teaching, even after the Romans conquered the Greeks. Asclepiades of Bithynia (in modern-day Turkey) lived from 124BC until 40BC. He took Greek ideas about medicine to Rome. He did not believe in the healing power of nature, nor that humours caused disease. He recommended treatments such as poultices, massage, good diet and plenty of fresh air. Asclepiades was also the first to study mental illness. He prescribed music, occupational therapy (work) and exercise, together with plenty of wine to sedate people (make them calm or sleepy).

The Romans employed mostly Greek doctors. Even then, many people preferred to treat ailments themselves with herbs and charms. Cornelius Celsus, a Roman nobleman, wrote a detailed history of medicine in about 25BC. Doctors used this work up until the 1400s. It described diseases of the eyes, nose and ears, hernias, bladder stones and other common conditions.

▼ CUPPING
The Romans and Greeks drew foul humours out of the body in a process called cupping. A piece of lint was set alight and placed inside a cup, which was pressed against the skin, an open wound, or a surgical cut. As the oxygen was used up the cup became a vacuum (airless space). This created suction (like in a vacuum cleaner) that sucked out the 'vicious humours.'

LEARNING FROM COMBAT
According to Galen, much disease resulted from an excess of blood, one of the four humours. This surplus blood might putrefy (rot) in some part of the body, and should be removed by bloodletting. Sometimes patients were even bled until they became unconscious. Like Galen's other teachings, bloodletting persisted until the 1800s, resulting in many unnecessary deaths.

◀ ROMAN GLADIATOR
Before moving to Rome, Galen was physician to the gladiators in Alexandria. He must have gained useful experience of anatomy and surgery by treating these professional fighters.

▲ BATTLEFIELD MEDICINE
The Roman army was the first to use doctors on the battlefield. They set up field hospitals to provide instant medical care.

▶ SURGICAL HOOK
Roman surgeons used a bronze hook to tease apart the tissue during an operation. This kept the blood vessels and muscles out of the way and gave the doctor a clear view.

◀ PUBLIC BATHS
The Romans took great care of their bodies. They spent many hours in the public baths, soaking in hot water or enjoying a massage. This helped them to avoid infections caused by poor hygiene.

▼ ROMAN AQUEDUCT
Clean water supplies were an important public health measure introduced by the Romans. Aqueducts were bridges that carried supplies of fresh water from sources many kilometres away.

During the 1st and 2nd centuries AD, many Greek doctors journeyed to Rome. Claudius Galen moved to Rome in AD162 and went on to become the physician to five different Roman emperors. He was so influential that his writings were accepted for the next 1,500 years. Galen developed Hippocrates' theories about humours but, unlike the Greeks, he believed in experimenting.

Human dissection was not permitted, so Galen learned about anatomy by dissecting monkeys and other animals. As a result, many of his assumptions were later proved wrong. Galen showed that blood ebbs and flows as the heart beats, but he never realized that it flows around the body. He wrote at least 350 books about medicine, some describing very complex operations. Galen's works were so respected that they went unchallenged for centuries. Even his mistakes were widely accepted up until the 1500s, when doctors

began to experiment once more.

While Greek influence accounted for most medical advances in Rome, the Romans made important advances in maintaining public health, which reduced infectious disease. Fresh water was piped into the cities and public baths were built. There was proper sanitation and refuse collection. Clinics and hospitals were built and there were also army doctors who treated soldiers' battle wounds.

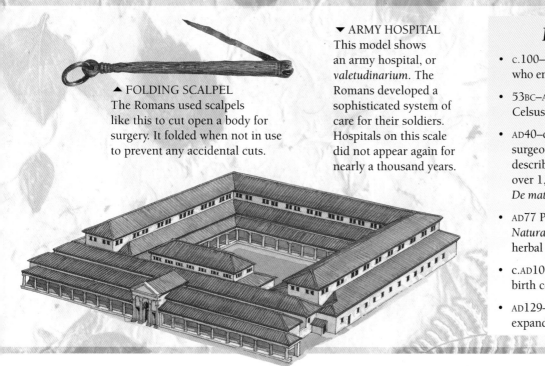

▲ FOLDING SCALPEL
The Romans used scalpels like this to cut open a body for surgery. It folded when not in use to prevent any accidental cuts.

▼ ARMY HOSPITAL
This model shows an army hospital, or *valetudinarium*. The Romans developed a sophisticated system of care for their soldiers. Hospitals on this scale did not appear again for nearly a thousand years.

Key Dates

- c.100–44BC Life of Julius Caesar, who employs doctors in the army.

- 53BC–AD7 Life of Cornelius Celsus, author of *De medicina*.

- AD40–c.90 Life of Nero's army surgeon, Dioscorides, who describes around 600 plants and over 1,000 drugs in his book, *De materia medica*.

- AD77 Pliny the Elder's *Historia Naturalis* describes surgery and herbal remedies.

- c.AD100 Soranus writes about birth control and pregnancy.

- AD129–216 Life of Galen, who expands on Greek writings.

The Arab World

▲ SURGICAL SCISSORS
Scissors were developed as a more precise way than knives or scalpels to cut through tissue.

▶ AVICENNA
Avicenna was a Persian doctor working within the Arab Empire. His book, the Canon of Medicine, *was used across the Middle East and Europe for centuries.*

DURING THE PERIOD of the Byzantine Empire (AD300–1453), the works of Greek and Roman doctors were collected together. Some appeared in the languages used at the fringes of the empire, such as Persian and Syrian.

Meanwhile the Arab Empire was growing in power and influence. It conquered Persia and Syria. At first, the Arabs preferred their own traditional remedies, but as the power of the Islamic religion increased in the Arab Empire, many traditional treatments were lost. Doctors began to turn to ancient Greek ideas and translated Greek texts into Arabic. This meant that ancient Greek learning spread throughout the Arab Empire, into Europe and around the Mediterranean.

Important places of learning sprang up in Baghdad, Cairo and Damascus in the Middle East, and in Toledo, Cordoba and Seville in what is now Spain. Arab scientists and doctors published copies of the early medical works. Some of these were later translated into Latin and used in European medical schools from the 1200s.

Arab medicine did not contribute much new knowledge, but Arab writers made detailed descriptions of diseases and their diagnoses. Surgery suffered in early years, because dissection was banned, so little was known about anatomy. However, an Arab surgeon in Cordoba wrote a text on surgical techniques and others developed techniques for surgery on the eye and the internal organs. The Arabs were interested in alchemy (trying to transform cheap metals into gold, and searching for a source of eternal life). Their alchemical experiments led them to find many

MEDICAL PIONEERS

Not all of the medical scholars were Arabs. Many were Persians, Jews or Christians living within the Arab Empire. Rhazes was a Persian who put together a huge medical compendium. Maimonides was a Jewish doctor born in the 1100s. He became physician to the Saracen ruler Saladin. His extensive writings on medicine were based on Greek ideas.

◀ RHAZES
The Persian physician Rhazes was born about AD865. He wrote more than 200 books on a huge range of subjects. He was admired for his medical care of the poor.

▲ EYE SURGERY
Cataracts is an eye condition that clouds the lens of the eye and eventually leads to blindness. Arab physicians developed a technique for dislodging the clouded lens and pushing it clear of the field of vision. This allowed some degree of sight to be restored.

drugs by accident. Alchemists also developed techniques for purifying chemicals that are still used today. Arab pharmacists compiled long lists of herbal remedies, gathered from the places they conquered. Some describe more than 3,000 different drugs, some of which were very unusual. The real value of Arab writings, however, was how carefully they recorded information. These great works were painstakingly copied and circulated throughout the Arab Empire.

◀ MIXING MEDICINES
Persian and Arab apothecaries (pharmacists or dispensing chemists) developed a variety of methods for preparing medicines. These Persians are boiling ingredients over burning coals.

▼ PESTLE AND MORTAR
The simplest way to make up a herbal medicine was to grind its ingredients together using a pestle and mortar. This made a powder that could be mixed with water and drunk, or made into a paste or ointment. They are still in common use today.

▼ MEDICINE IN THE ARAB EMPIRE
The Arab Empire spread widely around the Mediterranean and the Middle East and adopted the traditional remedies of the regions it conquered. Arab scholars preserved ancient Greek and Roman traditions and wrote down the newest medical discoveries.

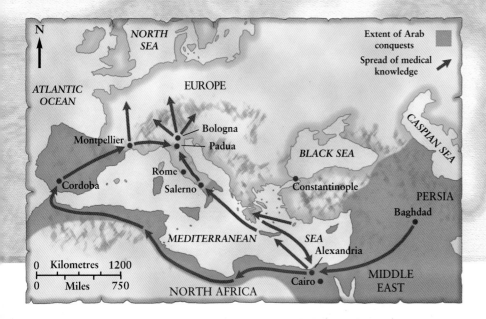

Extent of Arab conquests ▒

Spread of medical knowledge →

Key Dates

- AD620s Muhammad founds Islam.

- AD832 Baghdad is established as a place of learning.

- AD850 Muslim scholar at-Tabari compiles medical writings of Greece, Rome, Persia and India.

- c.AD865–928 Life of Rhazes.

- AD980–1037 Life of Avicenna.

- 1174 Maimonides is appointed as court physician to Saladin.

- 1236 Christians gain Cordoba.

- 1258 Mongol warriors sack Baghdad. Medical information preserved by the Arabs begins to flow back to the West.

Galen's Legacy

▲ URINE GAZING
During the 1200s and 1300s, there were few ways to diagnose a disease. One method was to examine the patient's urine. Its appearance and even its taste were carefully noted.

▶ MEDICAL GIANTS
In this edition of Galen's works published in 1528, Galen is shown with two other medical geniuses. Hippocrates is on the left and Avicenna on the right.

AFTER THE EMPEROR Constantine made Christianity the official religion of the Roman Empire, the power of Greek medicine and Galenic teaching began to fade. Once more, religion became more influential than practical medicine. Sickness was often seen as punishment from God for past sins. Prayer and pilgrimages to holy relics were the recommended cures for most diseases and cults of healing saints sprang up.

The Church's opinion of medicine was summed up by St Bernard, who lived from AD1090 until 1153. He said that going to the doctor was not a proper way to behave. Trying to cure a disease was seen as interfering with God's punishment. A dying person was more likely to call a priest than a doctor.

Christian saints became associated with different diseases. St Christopher dealt with epilepsy, St Roch was the patron saint of plague victims, St Apollonia looked after those with toothache and St Margaret kept women safe during childbirth.

However, the sick did receive some practical care. Many monasteries offered care of the sick. Hospitals were built across Europe, often alongside healing shrines (holy places). Special hospitals were built for lepers, who were treated with especial horror and considered 'unclean.'

Medical knowledge began to improve in the AD1000s, when a

FALSE BELIEFS

Throughout the Middle Ages, superstition formed part of medical practice. Herbals were books that listed the medicinal properties of plants. A few of these did have the promised effect, but most were useless. Bleeding, the use of leeches, enemas and deliberate vomiting were all recommended. Following the ideas of Hippocrates, these methods were thought to restore the balance of the humours.

◀ LUNGWORT
Many plants were used in medicine on the basis of their appearance. This practice was known as the doctrine of signatures. The leaves of lungwort were thought to look like the lung, so this plant was used to treat lung disease.

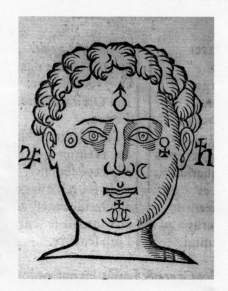

◀ ASTROLOGY
Astrology was thought to show a link between diseased body parts, different planets and star signs, and parts of the body. This is a chart showing planets' influences on the head.

▶ PURGING
Powerful drugs were given to cause vomiting. This purging and was believed to rid the body of poisons.

small group of doctors began work at Salerno, in Italy. They formed an influential medical school and revived ancient ideas, especially those of Galen. People assumed Galen's teachings were accurate, even though some were changed or missed out in translation and others had been wrong in the first place. Doctors treated their patients with diets and drugs, many of which were imported from the East.

Surgery became a separate branch of medicine and was carried out by barber-surgeons. Barber-surgeons provided a range of services. They cut hair, pulled out teeth, gave enemas (injected fluids into the rectum) and let blood.

At least one Greek technique was challenged. Hippocrates had recommended leaving open wounds to become septic. Henri de Mondeville, a French surgeon who lived from 1260 until 1320, had different ideas. He advised closing the wound as soon as possible and keeping it dry and covered to prevent infection. Thanks to de Mondeville, many limbs and lives were saved.

▲ LEECHES
Bloodletting was a treatment for most illnesses. People often used freshwater leeches to suck out the blood. Recently, the use of leeches has been reintroduced as a way to reduce serious bruising.

▼ CAUTERIZING IRON
To stop bleeding, medieval doctors used to apply a red-hot iron to coagulate (thicken) the blood. This caused agonizing pain. Cauterization was not very hygienic and many wounds became infected.

▼ POMANDER
In medieval times, people thought that foul smells spread disease. Many carried scented pomanders about with them to drive these smells away. The simplest pomanders were oranges stuck with aromatic spices called cloves.

▲ HOLY EYES
St Lucy of Syracuse became the patron saint of eye disease. According to legend, she plucked out her own eyes but they grew back. Many sick people still pray to saints.

Key Dates

- 1100–1300 Medical schools and hospitals are founded throughout Europe.

- 1100s Trotula joins the Salerno medical school. She writes the first complete work on women's health and another on skin disease.

- 1200s–1300s Physicians and surgeons begin to form into professional organizations.

- 1215 Pope Innocent III decrees that all doctors must be approved by the Church and bans lepers from the Church.

- 1260–1320 Henri de Mondeville recommends closing wounds.

Renaissance Discoveries

THE RENAISSANCE was the period in European history that lasted from the 1400s until the 1600s. Before then, European medicine had been based on theory rather than practice. Then Renaissance scientists and physicians began to question the old Greek writings on medicine. Some brave individuals even challenged the Church's teachings on the effect of the soul on the body. This change of approach was not the result of renewed interest in Greek and Roman medicine. It was led by people who rejected tradition and wished to discover and investigate. Scientists

▲ THERMOMETER
Unlike a modern one, this mercury thermometer from the 1400s had to be kept in the patient's mouth for up to 25 minutes.

▶ VESALIUS
This picture by Eduoard Hamman was made during the 1800s. It shows how Vesalius dissected human bodies so that he could make extremely detailed anatomical drawings.

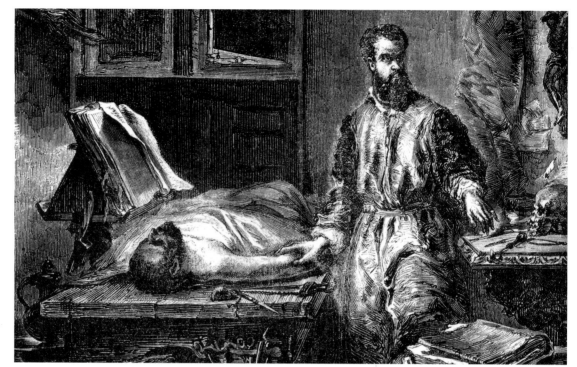

MEDICAL REVOLUTIONARIES
The ideas of Hippocrates and Galen had been followed for so long without question, that it was difficult to abandon them. New ideas did not always offer a comforting solution to medical problems and many traditional doctors did not welcome them. Despite opposition, revolutionary scientists and doctors persevered and made some ground-breaking discoveries.

▶ PARACELSUS
Paracelsus was a Swiss doctor. His belief in alchemy, which was unfashionable at the time, nevertheless led him to discover important new drugs. In this way, Paracelsus pioneered chemical treatment of disease.

▼ MARCELLO MALPIGHI
The Italian biologist and doctor Malpighi was able to complete part of the story of blood circulation. He discovered the capillary vessels that link arteries and veins, which Harvey had been unable to see.

▲ WILLIAM HARVEY
Harvey was the first person to prove that the heart pumped blood through the body, which he did by identifying the direction of blood flow. He even demonstrated his discovery to King Charles I of England.

started to dissect human bodies. The first anatomists were puzzled to see that their findings did not match Galen's descriptions. Their new knowledge led to great advances in surgery.

The greatest revolution in the understanding of anatomy and physiology came from the work of the Flemish physician Andreas Vesalius. In 1543 he published his detailed drawings of dissections of the human body. Vesalius was Professor of Anatomy at the University of Padua, Italy. One of his successors, Hieronymus Fabricius, studied the function of the valves in the veins and established that they made the blood flow in one direction. He tried to blend his findings with those of Galen, so he did not realize that the blood circulated around the body. One of his students, an Englishman called William Harvey, was able to contribute to the story by demonstrating the circulation of the blood. However, even Harvey missed the final link because he did not realize how blood passes from the arteries to the veins.

As people realized that many ancient manuscripts and descriptions were inaccurate, they collected new descriptions of medicinal plants in books called herbals. This led to the discovery of many plants and drugs previously unknown in Western Europe. These included the rhubarb root (first described in a Chinese herbal over 4,000 years earlier), which was used to cleanse the bowels. Explorers to the New World, especially the Spanish and Portuguese, brought back amazing new plants, while visitors to the Far East brought back new drugs and remedies, too.

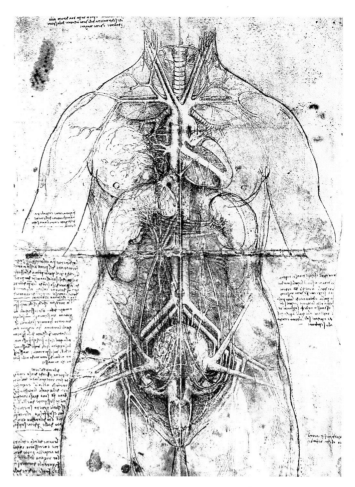

▲ THE MAJOR ORGANS OF THE BODY
Leonardo da Vinci's anatomical drawings were undoubted works of art. Often, however, they were highly inaccurate. Da Vinci made guesses rather than performing detailed dissections himself.

▲ AMBROISE PARÉ
Paré was a French army surgeon who came to realize that cauterizing wounds often resulted in the patient dying. He developed a gentler form of dressing and tying off of severed blood vessels, making a huge advance in surgical care.

▼ GIROLAMO FRACASTORO
This Italian formulated the idea that infection could spread from one person to another by physical contact, or through the air. He guessed that this might be caused by tiny living organisms, which he called 'seeds.' However, he could not prove his theory, so it was largely dismissed.

Key Dates

- 1482 Pope Sixtus IV allows the dissection of executed criminals.

- 1527 Paracelsus burns the books of Avicenna and Galen.

- 1537 Ambroise Paré develops his concept of wound care.

- 1540 Barber-Surgeons' Company is founded in England.

- 1546 Fracastoro publishes his theories on germs and disease.

- 1628 William Harvey publishes his theory of blood circulation.

- 1661 Marcello Malpighi publishes his theory on the circulation of the blood through the lungs.

Plague and Pestilence

▲ FLEA
Bubonic plague is spread by the bite of a flea that has fed on the blood of an infected rat. European towns and cities were infested with rats during the 1300s and 1400s.

IN AD540 A TERRIBLE DISEASE broke out in Europe. This epidemic is known as Justinian's Plague, after the Byzantine emperor at the time. So many people died that the his empire was almost destroyed. During the 1300s, the plague reappeared in Europe. This outbreak is known as the Black Death, or bubonic plague. Between 1348 and 1351 it killed around 20 million people.

The plague had reached Constantinople in 1347, carried by traders fleeing from the advance of Mongol warriors from Asia. They brought the disease with them from the steppes (grasslands) where they originally lived. Although humans can catch it, plague is a disease of rodents, and especially of the black rat. Infected rats were bitten by fleas that fed on their blood. When the host rat died, the fleas looked for a new source of food. They bit people, who then became infected with the plague.

Infected people developed swellings around the neck, armpits and groin, and bled beneath the skin, producing sores called buboes. They died at such a rate that bodies were just dumped in huge pits. Doctors were helpless to treat the plague. Isolating infected people did not help, because rats were everywhere. Once most of the rats died, the plague slowly vanished. However, it came back again at intervals. There was another serious outbreak during the 1800s. The plague is still around today, for example in the USA.

Bubonic plague was not the only disease to strike Europe in the Middle Ages. Leprosy was common.

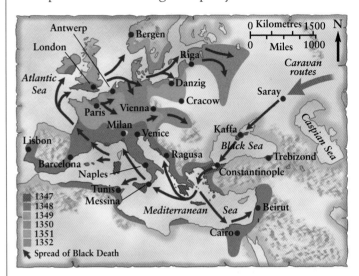

▲ SPREAD OF THE PLAGUE
In 1347 the bubonic plague arrived at the trading post of Kaffa (modern-day Feodosiya, in Ukraine). Merchants unwittingly carried the disease to Constantinople. From there, it soon spread rapidly throughout Europe.

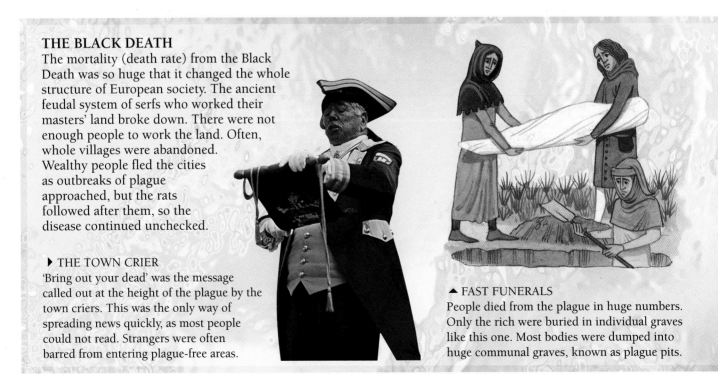

THE BLACK DEATH
The mortality (death rate) from the Black Death was so huge that it changed the whole structure of European society. The ancient feudal system of serfs who worked their masters' land broke down. There were not enough people to work the land. Often, whole villages were abandoned. Wealthy people fled the cities as outbreaks of plague approached, but the rats followed after them, so the disease continued unchecked.

▶ THE TOWN CRIER
'Bring out your dead' was the message called out at the height of the plague by the town criers. This was the only way of spreading news quickly, as most people could not read. Strangers were often barred from entering plague-free areas.

▲ FAST FUNERALS
People died from the plague in huge numbers. Only the rich were buried in individual graves like this one. Most bodies were dumped into huge communal graves, known as plague pits.

▶ THE TRIUMPH
OF DEATH
*Pieter Bruegel painted his
Triumph of Death in
about 1562. It features
nightmarish skeletons
and gives some idea of the
hysterical fear caused by
the plague. The title of
the painting refers to the
commonly-held belief that
the Black Death was a
victory for the forces of evil.*

▼ PLAGUE VICTIM
*This illustration appeared in
the Toggenberg Bible in the
1400s. It clearly shows the
huge buboes, or swellings,
that covered a plague
victim's body.*

Although the disease is not very infectious, lepers were feared and treated as social outcasts. There were also epidemics of cholera and typhoid. Cholera was especially feared because it killed most people who caught it and no one understood what caused it. It was caused by sewage and rubbish in rivers. People picked up the bacteria causing these diseases from contaminated drinking water and food.

Medicine was powerless against these epidemics, so prayer was the only option for the terrified people when disease broke out.

▶ PLAGUE HOUSE
The doors of houses where plague victims lived were marked with a red cross. Some houses were sealed up, even if there were healthy people still living inside.

◀ DR DEATH
Plague doctors offered to cure or prevent the disease. To keep themselves clear of infection they wore strange costumes. They stuffed their headdresses with sweet-smelling herbs and carried amulets and pomanders.

Key Dates

- AD540 Justinian's Plague attacks Constantinople.

- 1347 Plague reaches the Black Sea coast. It spreads all over Europe from Constantinople within two years.

- 1349 Jews are blamed for the plague and massacred in Strasbourg, Mainz and Frankfurt.

- 1377 The port of Dubrovnik quarantines itself, followed by the ports of Venice and Pisa in Italy, and Marseilles, in France.

- 1665 The Great Plague attacks London. King Charles II and his court flee to the countryside.

Making a Diagnosis

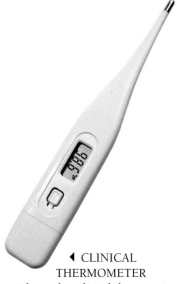

◀ CLINICAL THERMOMETER
The modern digital thermometer is quick and easy to use, and is also extremely accurate. It does not contain the poisonous mercury used in traditional thermometers, which were fragile and easily broken.

D IAGNOSIS IS THE skill of identifying a disease. It is carried out by observing signs and symptoms of the illness. Until recently there were few medical tests to help a doctor identify a disease. Instead, doctors would talk to their patients, examine them and looked at how they behaved.

In Greece, at the time of Hippocrates, doctors tried to identify their patient's disease so they could reach their prognosis (say how the disease would develop). A doctor's reputation rested on how accurately

he predicted whether the patient would recover or die. Hippocrates taught that every single observation could be significant. Greek doctors used all of their senses in making their diagnosis. Touch, taste, sight, hearing and smell could all provide valuable clues. These principles still apply for modern doctors.

By Galen's time, taking the pulse had become a part of diagnosis. Galen gave instructions on how to take the

▶ USING THE STETHOSCOPE
The stethoscope introduced by Laënnec in 1819 was awkward to use, because it was rigid. Unlike the modern stethoscope, which has a bendy rubber tube, it was not easy to move around in order to detect sounds in different areas.

TOOLS OF THE TRADE
Diagnosis improved with the invention of instruments that allowed the doctor to find out what was going on inside the body. A whole range of new observations could be made, and these were added to the findings from old methods, such as interviewing the patient. Better measurements of pulse rate, blood pressure and temperature all helped towards accurate diagnosis.

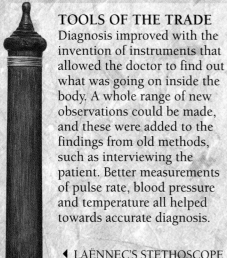

◀ LAËNNEC'S STETHOSCOPE
In 1819 the French physician René Laënnec introduced the first stethoscope. This wooden device, almost 23cm/9in long, amplified the sounds of the chest.

▼ THE STETHOSCOPE TODAY
The modern stethoscope is a simple lightweight device. It allows doctors and nursing staff to listen to the sounds of the lungs and the heart. It often gives an early warning of illness.

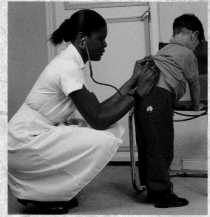

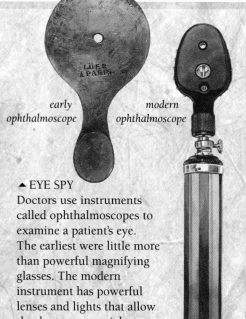

early ophthalmoscope   *modern ophthalmoscope*

▲ EYE SPY
Doctors use instruments called ophthalmoscopes to examine a patient's eye. The earliest were little more than powerful magnifying glasses. The modern instrument has powerful lenses and lights that allow the doctor to see right to the back of the eyeball.

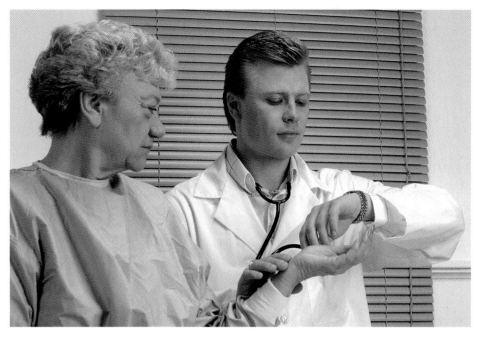

pulse. The findings could be described as 'fast' or 'normal.'

In the Arab world, diagnosis involved careful examination of the affected parts, checking the pulse and examining the urine. Arab doctors did not disclose their findings to anyone else in case they frightened the patient.

In most of Europe, diagnosis was rather haphazard, because disease was seen as a punishment from God. This meant its cause could not be questioned and the disease could not be treated, except with prayer. Sometimes the diagnosis was obvious to all, such as in cases of leprosy or plague, but even then the doctor was not able to cure the patient.

It was not until the 1700s that real advances were made in the art of diagnosis. In 1761, a Viennese doctor called Leopold Auenbrugger discovered that thumping on a patient's chest produced sounds which could indicate lung disease. The technique was reluctantly

accepted and is still in use today. However, most doctors did not perform physical examinations, and still formed their diagnosis by interviewing the patient. Auscultation (sounding the chest) improved with the invention of the stethoscope in 1816. This also allowed doctors to hear the heart properly, and diagnose different heart diseases.

Examination of the urine was a popular method of diagnosis for all sorts of disease. Its appearance, smell and even its taste were thought to reveal the state of the patient's health. Urine tests are still used in some forms of diagnosis today, for example to identify diabetes or pregnancy.

▲ COUNTING THE BEATS
Taking a person's pulse tells the doctor how fast the heart is beating. With each heartbeat, the arteries bulge slightly. The arteries at the wrist are very close to the skin surface, so the doctor can feel them bulge with his or her fingertip.

▲ UNDER PRESSURE
The sphygmomanometer is used to measure blood pressure. First the doctor puts an inflatable sleeve on the patient's arm. This is pumped up to close off the blood flow through the arteries. As the sleeve is slowly deflated, the device measures the blood pressure.

▼ BLOOD CHEMISTRY
Blood tests are used to measure changes in the chemical make up of the blood. These changes can indicate that a person is suffering from an infection, diabetes or some other hormonal disorder, or that a woman is pregnant.

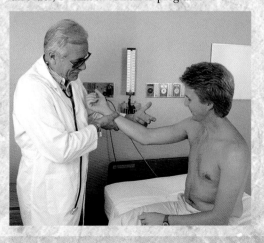

Key Dates

- 1714 Gabriel Fahrenheit invents the mercury thermometer.

- 1761 Leopold Auenbrugger publishes his findings on sounding the chest.

- 1819 René Laënnec introduces the first stethoscope.

- 1851 Hermann von Helmholtz invents the ophthalmoscope.

- 1868 Carl Wunderlich promotes widespread use of the thermometer.

- 1895 Wilhelm Röntgen discovers x-rays.

- 1896 Scipione Riva-Rocci invents the sphygmomanometer.

The Rise of Surgery

▲ JOHN HUNTER
Born in Scotland in 1728, John Hunter was very important to modern surgery. He changed people's views so that they saw it as a proper medical discipline. He put together a huge collection of medical specimens, which today is in the Hunterian Museum, in Glasgow.

SURGERY IS PROBABLY the oldest medical skill. Even pressing a hand over a cut to stop it bleeding is a form of surgery. Prehistoric skeletons show signs of bone-setting to repair broken limbs, and holes drilled into skulls in the process of trepanning. Some ancient civilizations carried out very sophisticated surgery, with operations on the eyes, and even on the intestines. However, during the Middle Ages, the skill was almost lost. Surgery was not taught in most European medical schools. It was left to barbers and other unskilled people to carry out surgery, usually as a last resort. During the Renaissance, there were attempts to improve matters. The United Company of Barber-Surgeons was set up in London in 1540 to give guidelines to people carrying out operations. However, most patients still died through infections due to lack of hygiene.

▶ SURGERY IN THE ROUND
This photograph, taken in 1898, shows surgery being performed at the Bellevue Hospital, New York. Fellow surgeons and medical students look on, so that they can learn the latest surgical techniques.

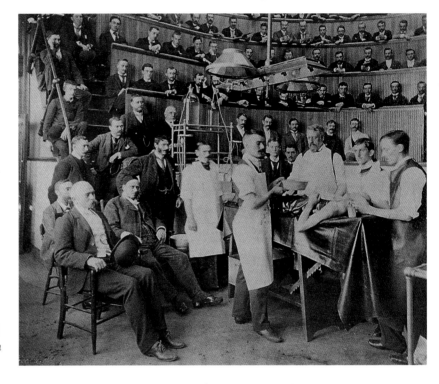

EARLY SURGERY
Surgery was carried out in ancient Mesopotamia as long ago as 2000BC, and in India in 100BC. The Indian surgeons were especially skilful and left behind detailed descriptions of delicate operations to remove cataracts from the eye. In ancient China, however, any invasion of the body was discouraged and surgery was seldom carried out. Advanced surgery was performed by the ancient Greeks and the Romans, and spread into the Arab Empire, eventually returning to Europe much later.

▼ HUA TUO
Surgical treatment was discouraged in ancient China. Its only record is of Hua Tuo operating on the arm of General Kuan Yun. Hua Tuo was executed for treason when he offered to perform a trepanning operation on Prince Tsao Tsao. The prince suspected a plot to murder him.

◀ BLEEDING A PATIENT
Bloodletting was one of the earliest and most common forms of surgery. In later times it was carried out by barber-surgeons. Bloodletting was used to treat almost all diseases. Patients were usually already very ill. The loss of blood often weakened them so much that they died.

In 1547, the French surgeon Ambroise Paré abandoned the traditional, agonizing cauterization of wounds with a red-hot iron. He found that he could tie off the blood vessels to prevent blood loss, with far less shock and mortality in his patients. It was another two centuries before any further advances were made.

By the 1700s, improved knowledge of anatomy meant that the removal of cancers and bladder stones were common operations. Amputations were carried out in less than five minutes to minimize pain and shock. Patients were sedated (quietened) with opium or alcohol and held down by attendants. However, many still died due to infection caused during surgery.

From the 1760s the British surgeon John Hunter turned surgery from amateur butchery into a scientific profession. He lectured, wrote widely, and collected huge numbers of medical specimens. Hunter was an expert dissector. As the number of hospitals had increased, so had the number of unclaimed dead bodies, which could be sent to the anatomy schools and used for training student surgeons.

Once pain and infection could be controlled, surgery became less risky. Operations became common for minor problems. Appendicitis had been recognized back in the 1500s, but surgery to remove the appendix was regarded as very dangerous. Then, in 1902, Frederic Treves drained an abscess on the appendix of the Prince of Wales, just before he was crowned Edward VIII. This won Treves a knighthood and, from then on, surgery to remove the appendix became highly fashionable.

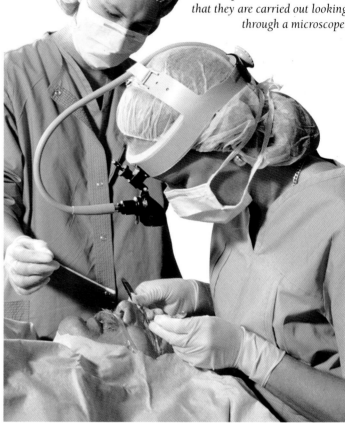

▼ EYE OPERATION
Modern surgery demands very precise instruments. This eye surgeon is using a scalpel that has a tiny blade made from diamond, which is extremely sharp. The doctor sees into the eye by means of a powerful magnifier. Some operations are so delicate that they are carried out looking through a microscope.

▲ LOSING A LEG
Amputations were a brutal business. They had to be carried out very swiftly so the patients would not die from bleeding and shock. In this picture, printed in 1618, the barber-surgeon already has cauterizing irons heating in the fire, ready to seal the wound.

▼ BLOOD STOPPER
The tourniquet was developed to stop blood loss after an amputation. The strap was fastened tightly around the limb above the place where the cut was to be made. Then the screw was tightened down to squeeze the arteries and cut off the blood flow.

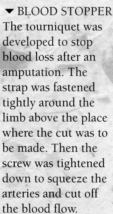

▲ SURGICAL SAW
At first, ordinary carpenters' saws were used for amputations. Later, specialized surgical saws were produced.

Key Dates

- AD600s The Ayurvedic *Sushruta-Samhita* describes over 120 types of steel surgical instrument.

- 1728–1793 Life of John Hunter, who revolutionizes the teaching and practice of surgery.

- 1793 French army surgeon Dominique-Jean Larrey introduces the first ambulance service, *Ambulances Volantes*.

- 1809 American Ephraim McDowell pioneers gynaecological surgery when he removes a growth from a woman's ovary.

- 1902 Frederic Treves treats the Prince of Wales' appendicitis.

Germ-free and Pain-free

▲ KEEPING CLEAN
Washing the hands is still one of the most important ways to limit the spread of infection, both in hospitals and in the home. Modern surgical staff use antibacterial soap to prevent infection.

▶ IGNAZ SEMMELWEISS
Semmelweiss realized that lack of hygiene was causing many deaths among his patients so he insisted on rigorous washing. His views were considered outrageous and he was forced out of his hospital in Vienna.

SURGERY IN THE 1600s was a very dangerous business. There was no concept of hygiene. Surgeons worked in their normal clothes, which became splashed with blood. They used instruments in consecutive operations without any attempt at cleaning. Childbirth fever was a particular hazard, killing many women within a few days of giving birth. A Hungarian doctor, Ignaz Semmelweiss, realized that patients were more likely to suffer infection after being examined by medical students who had been carrying out dissections. He saw that when students had not visited the dissection rooms, infection did not occur. As a result, Semmelweiss insisted on high standards of hygiene in his hospital, and this cut the death rate dramatically. He

was violently opposed by many medical colleagues, however, and eventually had to leave his practice in Vienna.

At this time no one realized that microbes spread disease. It was not until the 1860s that Louis Pasteur discovered bacterial infection. The British surgeon Joseph Lister made the next major advance. He was alarmed at how many people died of severe bone fractures. Lister observed that if a bone was broken without penetrating the skin, infection seldom occurred. If a bone fragment punctured the skin, exposing it to the air, there was usually an infection, and this led to amputation or death.

When Lister found out about Pasteur's work, he realized that it was not air that caused the problem, but bacteria contaminating the wound. Lister had heard that carbolic acid could be used to kill bacteria in sewage, so he tried spraying a mist of diluted carbolic acid on wounds. His experiment had dramatic results. Out of his first 11 patients, only one died. This discovery was resisted at first, but as it became accepted it was possible to carry out

KILLING THE PAIN
Anaesthesia has a long history. The ancient Greeks used drugs to provide pain relief. By the 1800s, opium was widely used as a soporific (to make the patient sleepy). Alcohol was also used in surgery to help the patient relax. Ether and nitrous oxide were the first modern anaesthetics. They were introduced at about the same time and were both inhaled. Shortly afterwards, chloroform was introduced. After initial resistance, all three of these anaesthetics were enthusiastically accepted and became very widely used.

▼ WILLIAM MORTON
Morton was an American dentist who experimented with the effects of ether as an anaesthetic. In 1846 he anaesthetized a patient for the surgeon John Collins Warren.

▲ FIRST FAILURE
In 1848, Hannah Greener became the first person to die from the poisonous effects of chloroform. Greener had only had a minor operation to remove a toenail.

▼ CHLOROFORM MASK
Chloroform and ether were both applied by soaking a cloth mask. The mask's wire frame closely covered the nose and mouth so that the chloroform or ether fumes were breathed in by the patient.

routine operations with hardly any risk to the patient. Asepsis (keeping free from infection) was safer than allowing a bacterial infection to take hold and then trying to treat it with antiseptics. To achieve this surgeons tried to keep bacteria away from wounds by sterilizing their instruments and wearing masks and gowns.

At about the same time that asepsis was discovered, several doctors discovered how pain could be relieved by the use of anaesthetics. In 1846 the American dentist Thomas Morton showed how ether could be used to eliminate pain during surgery, while John Warren also experimented with the use of nitrous oxide (laughing gas). Nitrous oxide had been used for a while as a party novelty. Breathing in the gas made people collapse in fits of giggles. Chloroform was another form of anaesthetic. After John Snow gave it to Queen Victoria during the birth of Prince Leopold, its use became more widespread.

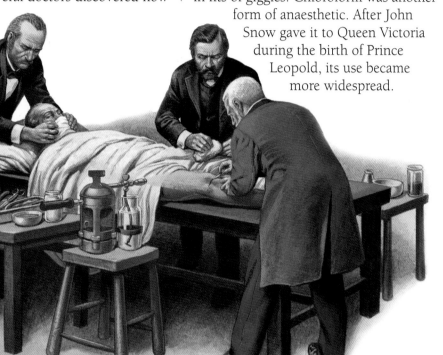

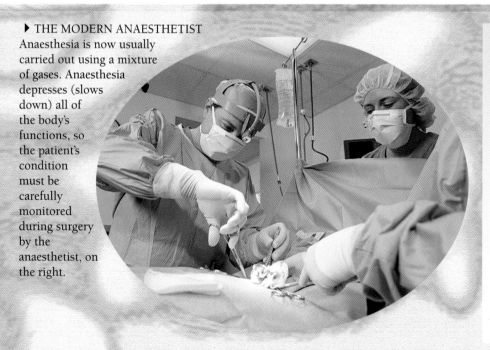

▲ STEAM SPRAY
Joseph Lister invented the carbolic steam spray. It produced a fine mist of mild carbolic acid in the operating room and killed bacteria. The death rate among Lister's patients fell from 50 per cent to 5 per cent.

◀ UNDER THE KNIFE
From the 1860s, operations were carried out in antiseptic conditions. A carbolic steam spray pumped an antibacterial mist into the room. Surgery was not only safer, it was more comfortable for the patient. Chloroform masks kept them unconscious during the operation.

▶ THE MODERN ANAESTHETIST
Anaesthesia is now usually carried out using a mixture of gases. Anaesthesia depresses (slows down) all of the body's functions, so the patient's condition must be carefully monitored during surgery by the anaesthetist, on the right.

Key Dates

- 1800 Humphrey Davy reports that nitrous oxide can produce unconsciousness.

- 1831 Chloroform is discovered.

- 1844 Horace Wells uses nitrous oxide to anaesthetize a patient.

- 1846 William Morton uses ether to anaesthetize a patient.

- 1847 Ignaz Semmelweiss makes his staff wash their hands.

- 1865 Joseph Lister uses his carbolic steam spray in surgery.

- 1884 Cocaine is used as a local anaesthetic, pain-killing drug.

- 1886 Aseptic surgery begins.

Quacks and Charlatans

KOLA MARQUE
This French poster is advertising a stimulant containing the drug cocaine. Some quack cures were completely useless. Others, such as Kola Marque, contained dangerous and addictive ingredients.

I T IS EASY FOR US to dismiss doctors in the past as being quacks or charlatans (people who swindled their patients by selling them useless cures). This was certainly true of some of them, but their strange activities need to be put into the context of the level of scientific learning of the time. For instance, it would not have been possible to convince Hippocrates or Galen about the existence of bacteria, or that bacteria cause disease, because it was only possible to see them through a microscope.

QUACK MEDICINES
Salespeople drew attention to their wares by any means at their disposal. Many wore outrageous and eye-catching outfits, and they all perfected their own style of patter (sales talk).

Although surgery could sometimes be effective, most medicine was not able to cure disease. Doctors were forced to desperate measures in order to find cures.

Sometimes a patient recovered by natural means, but then the experimental method used by the doctor would be accepted as a miracle cure.

Prayer and the use of holy relics might be dismissed as quack medicine, but they are still widely used today, along with the laying on of hands (blessing the patient) and other forms of therapy based upon spiritual cure.

In Britain, quackery flourished in the 1700s. Outlandish cures were sold on street corners and at fairs and markets. During the 1800s people realized that quacks were exploiting the sick with cures and treatments that had no value at all.

Medical associations, such as the Royal Colleges in Britain, were set up. These professional organizations kept out charlatans and regulated the activities of doctors who were members. They also checked that the doctors were skilled enough to

FALSE HOPES
As medicine becomes more advanced, cures that were once promoted by respectable doctors are rejected as quackery. For example, spa baths were a popular treatment in Western Europe around 1900. They are now less popular, and many doctors would consider their use to be a form of quack medicine. However, they are still mainstream practice in parts of Eastern Europe.

MUDBATHS
Baths in hot mud are widely used to treat diseases such as arthritis, especially in Eastern Europe. Elsewhere, mud treatments are considered harmless, but ineffective.

ELECTRICAL CORSETS
Electricity was considered a magical cure-all in the 1700s and 1800s. Electrical currents were applied to parts of the body to cure a whole range of conditions.

FRANZ MESMER
The German physician Franz Mesmer developed techniques for what we now call hypnosis (putting someone into a trance). He called his discovery animal magnetism, and used it to treat patients who suffered from hysteria. His cures sometimes worked, even though they were scientific nonsense. Eventually, Mesmer was exposed as a fraud.

◀ MORISON'S PILLS
During the 1800s, James Morison's Vegetable Universal Pills achieved huge commercial success throughout Europe and the USA. Commonly known as Morison's Pills, they were said to cure all sorts of disease, but were found to be merely a mixture of powerful laxatives. This cartoon from the period pokes fun at people who believed in such unreliable cures. It suggests that the man has taken so many Morison's Pills that they have taken root in his stomach and made his skin sprout with grass!

perform their job. Gradually, laws were passed to stop products being sold with outrageous promises.

Lydia Pinkham's Vegetable Compound, introduced in 1873, was one of the most popular quack remedies – probably beccause it contained huge quantities of alcohol. This was sold first as a treatment for 'female weaknesses' and later as a cure for just about anything.

In the USA, quacks advertised cancer cures at high prices. These were aimed at desperate cancer sufferers, willing to pay almost any price for life. Quacks had to pay heavy fines if they were caught, but the practice still exists. Since the 1970s many people dying from cancer have visited Mexico to buy a so-called cure called laetrile, which is in fact poisonous. The same happens with AIDS, where unscrupulous dealers sell dubious pills and potions to those infected with HIV.

◀ FRANZ GALL
The German doctor Franz Gall developed the concept of phrenology. Phrenology is a form of diagnosis based on examining the skull. Gall claimed that skull shape revealed the functions of parts of the brain. He 'read' the skull by feeling for bumps. Phrenology survived for many years, but it is no longer considered to have any use to medicine.

▼ PHRENOLOGY
This porcelain head is marked with the regions identified by Franz Gall. Each area was identified with an aspect of a person's personality or how they behave, such as secretiveness or wit.

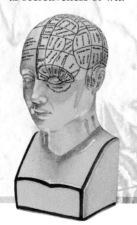

Key Dates

- 1700s Benjamin Franklin praises air bathing (sitting naked near an open window).

- 1775 Franz Mesmer develops his theory of animal magnetism.

- 1780 James Graham opens his Temple of Health in London.

- 1810s Franz Gall develops the concept of phrenology.

- 1970s Laetrile is promoted as a cure for cancer.

- 1991 The American Cancer Society declares laetrile is poisonous, but it remains on sale, especially on the Internet.

Public Health

▲ CHOLERA
This image from the 1800s shows cholera in the form of a spectre that descends on the Earth to claim its victims. More than 7,000 Londoners died in an outbreak in 1832.

PUBLIC HEALTH is not a new idea. The Romans understood the need for clean water supplies and built huge aqueducts to bring in water to the hearts of their cities, along with water pipes and public baths. They also constructed elaborate sewage systems to remove waste from their cities. The Romans were not even the first to build aqueducts. The Etruscans had started to build them in 312 BC.

Ancient Chinese and Indian religious writings had recommended good diet and hygiene to protect health, but in medieval Europe, all of this was forgotten. The Church frowned on washing, as it seemed too much like a bodily pleasure. There was no concept of hygiene, and sewage and rubbish were just thrown out into the street. It is no coincidence that during this period Europe was ravaged by plague, leprosy, tuberculosis (TB, also known as consumption),

typhoid and cholera. People thought that these diseases were spread by miasma (unpleasant smells). This idea probably did encourage some disposal of waste. The miasmic theory of infection persisted into the 1800s, until the effects of bacteria were finally demonstrated.

The cholera epidemics had already brought matters to a head. For centuries the River Thames had been London's sewer and source of drinking water. It was black and stinking, and finally everyone had had enough. The government commissioned a report from a civil servant called John Chadwick, which turned out to be the most influential document ever prepared on the subject of public health. It was published in 1842. The report described the probable causes of disease in the poorer parts of London, and also suggested practical ways to solve the problem. These public health measures included supplying houses with clean running water and proper sewage drainage.

Not long after this came the first proof of the risks from contaminated water, during a terrible cholera outbreak in 1854. John Snow, a London doctor, realized that many cholera cases were clustered in a small area near Broad Street. Investigation showed that they all drew their water from a public pump. Snow removed the pump handle, and within a few days the epidemic stopped. Even so, it took several years for the medical profession to accept that cholera was not spread by foul air, but by drinking water contaminated by sewage.

CLEAN SOLUTIONS
Flushing toilets and clean running water in the home remained novelties into the 1800s. Before then, people had to visit public pumps and taps for their water. In the late 1800s local authorities began to demolish the worst slums and replace them with better housing. By the 1900s children's health was improving. Schools provided meals for the poorest, and medical inspections allowed disease to be detected early on.

▶ FOUL WATERS
Dr John Snow started as a surgeon in Newcastle-upon-Tyne, England, and moved to London in 1836. After halting the cholera epidemic he recommended improvements in sewerage.

▶ WATER CLOSET
Flushing toilets, such as this one from the 1880s, were a great improvement in public health. The first toilets were often elaborately decorated and were almost works of art.

▲ AMERICAN SINK (1888)
The kitchen of the 1800s was not always very hygienic. Hot water on tap was a rare luxury. Cleanliness depended on having enough servants to scrub all the work surfaces and floors, which often carried germs.

▶ LONDON LIVING CONDITIONS
During the 1800s, living conditions for the poor were atrocious. They lived in cramped housing without proper sanitation. These people are going through the rubbish on the river. Such conditions provided an ideal breeding ground for disease.

▼ BUILDING A SEWER
Repeated outbreaks of disease finally led to the building of sewers, such as this one being dug in London in 1862. These enormous mains sewers were connected to outfalls far down the River Thames, where the tides could sweep the sewage away.

▲ ROYAL VICTORIA HOSPITAL, MONTREAL
Many hospitals were built in the 1800s, such as this one in Canada. These were often magnificent buildings, but as there were still few effective medical treatments, many patients came to hospital to die.

Key Dates

- c.1700BC King Minos of Crete has a flushing toilet in his palace.

- 312BC The Etruscans build the first aqueduct.

- AD300s Two-seater toilet, shaped like a temple, in use in Greece.

- c.1590 John Harrington invents a flushing toilet.

- 1770–1915 Development of the modern water closet, or toilet.

- 1854 John Snow shows dirty water is the cause of cholera.

- 1880s Most British cities have sewage treatment plants, after the Public Health Act of 1875.

Microbe Hunters

▲ BACTERIA
Researchers grow bacteria on agar jelly in petri dishes. They draw a contaminated glass rod across the surface of the jelly and the colonies grow in a streak along this line.

Back in the Renaissance, people had speculated that contact with an infected person might spread disease, but no one knew why. Then, in the early 1700s, the Dutch scientist Antonie van Leeuwenhoek described tiny animals that he saw when looking at body fluids under a microscope. These might, it was thought, be associated with disease.

Two hundred years later, the French scientist Louis Pasteur finally proved that microbes (germs) cause disease. First, he proved that microbes made milk sour and wine ferment. He also found that heat treatment killed off these microbes. This process, known as pasteurization, is still used to help preserve milk today. Pasteur went on to show how bacteria caused disease in chickens, and also caused anthrax, a severe infection that affects cattle and humans.

Robert Koch was a German doctor who was also studying anthrax. Using some of Koch's bacteria, Pasteur made a vaccine to prevent the disease in livestock. Even more importantly he went on to produce a vaccine for the killer disease rabies. Pasteur was, however, unable to find the organism that caused rabies, because it is a virus, invisible except under a high-powered electron microscope.

Koch was a very painstaking scientist who was aware of the

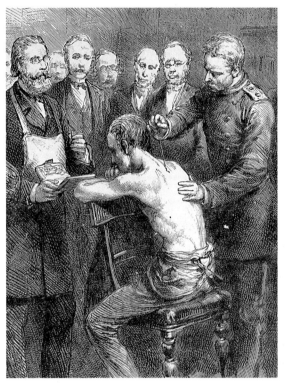

◀ ROBERT KOCH
Koch became famous as the conqueror of diphtheria. Here, he is examining a patient with TB. Koch managed to reveal the bacterium responsible for causing TB, but he failed to produce an effective vaccine against it.

ON THE TRAIL

Colonization (settlement) of the warmer parts of the world introduced Europeans to a whole range of tropical diseases, to which they had no natural immunity. West Africa, in particular, was nicknamed 'the white man's grave.' Malaria, yellow fever and many other tropical diseases spread by insect bites caused prolonged disease and death. It was not until 1897 that it was realized that a mosquito bite could spread malaria. Within a few years people discovered that bites from infected insects also caused sleeping sickness, plague and yellow fever.

▶ THE FIRST MICROSCOPE
Van Leeuwenhoek was an expert at making lenses. He developed the first practical microscope in 1671. He jealously hid his technique for making lenses, but he did share his discoveries by describing what he saw.

▲ MAGGOTS
In 1699 Francesco Redi showed that maggots did not appear on meat that had been kept free of flies. Before then, people had thought that maggots just appeared on decaying materials. We now know that the flies laid their eggs in the meat.

▼ RUDOLF VIRCHOW
Virchow demonstrated that disease did not arise spontaneously from humours, but that 'all cells come from cells.' In other words, bacteria give rise to more bacteria, rather than appearing on their own.

need to identify disease organisms accurately. He laid down rules for proving that a particular microbe is the cause of a disease that are still followed today. Koch said that a microbe must be present in every case of the disease. It must be grown experimentally and in laboratory animals, and it must also be found when the disease is transmitted to another animal. Following these rules, Koch was able to prove that tuberculosis (TB) was caused by a bacterium. Next he went to Egypt and India to study cholera. He proved that it, too, was caused by a bacterium. Koch discovered that it lived in the human gut and was spread by polluted water. By 1883 he had provided scientific evidence for John Snow's earlier findings on the causes of cholera. Koch went on to discover the organisms responsible for diphtheria, typhoid, leprosy and many other infections.

◄ LOUIS PASTEUR
Pasteur's experiments proved that life did not arise from nowhere. He explained how microbes are responsible for making things go off and also for diseases.

▼ GERM EXPERIMENT
Pasteur proved that microbes exist with this experiment. He heated a nutrient broth (a substance in which bacteria will grow) in a flask. This killed any microbes already there. He sealed the flask to stop any new microbes getting in. The broth did not spoil until he opened the flask and germs were allowed to enter it from the air.

▼ MOSQUITO
In 1897, Ronald Ross made the discovery of malaria parasites in an *Anopheles* mosquito. This finally proved the link between these insects and the killer disease.

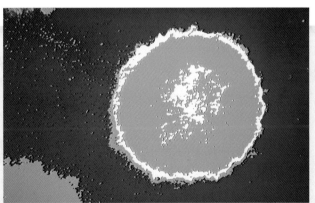

▲ HIV VIRUS
The discovery of the virus causing HIV in 1983 finally explained the mysterious appearance of AIDS. The HIV virus attacks and weakens the immune system. This allows the body to be attacked by other organisms and causes AIDS.

Key Dates

- 1673 Antonie van Leeuwenhoek describes the tiny life forms he has seen under a microscope.

- 1858 Rudolf Virchow states 'All cells come from cells.'

- 1878 Louis Pasteur presents his germ theory of infection to the French Academy of Medicine.

- 1882 Robert Koch isolates the tubercle bacillus that causes TB.

- 1883 Robert Koch isolates the bacterium that causes cholera.

- 1897 Ronald Ross explains how mosquitoes carry malaria.

- 1983 The HIV virus is discovered.

Immunization

▲ THE END OF
SMALLPOX
*One of the reasons for the
success in wiping out
smallpox was widespread
advertising explaining the
need for vaccination. This
example comes from China.*

THE STORY OF VACCINATION is largely also the story of smallpox. This viral disease killed or disfigured people throughout Europe and the American colonies, where it wiped out the civilizations of the Incas and Aztecs.

In 1717, Lady Mary Wortley Montagu, wife of the British Ambassador in Constantinople, reported that the Turks had a traditional method to prevent smallpox. They took pus from infected smallpox sores and scratched it into the skin of another person. This caused a mild infection that did not produce scarring. Most importantly, it seemed to make the person immune from later infection. Lady Montagu was confident enough to try this on her own child. Soon the method was used widely across Europe.

The next development came when Edward Jenner, a British physician, heard that milkmaids who caught cowpox from their cattle did not seem to catch smallpox. Cowpox was a mild disease. In 1796, Jenner injected a local boy with the cowpox virus. Six weeks later Jenner tried to infect the boy with smallpox. This experiment would have landed him in prison today. Fortunately the boy survived and the technique spread. Because smallpox does not infect any animals other than humans, it was possible to completely eradicate (wipe out) the disease by the end of the 1970s. Smallpox was the first organism that we have deliberately made extinct.

Immunization works by using the body's own natural

◀ EDWARD JENNER
This statue commemorates Jenner's first experimental vaccination of James Phelps with cowpox. This protected Phelps against smallpox infection.

PROTECTING PEOPLE

Viruses such as the influenza (flu) virus and HIV mutate, or change, very quickly, so the pattern of proteins on their surface also alters. This means that the body finds it difficult to produce strong immunity, because the disease is always changing. Other diseases such as polio and measles tend not to change, so vaccination provides powerful and permanent immunity.

▶ THE RABIES VACCINE
Louis Pasteur was able to produce rabies vaccines by growing the virus in rabbits' brains. Drying their brains and spinal cords for two weeks weakened the virus so much that it could be injected into people. This gave them immunity without them catching rabies.

▲ POLIO SUFFERER
In 1921, Franklin Roosevelt fell victim to polio. At the time, the disease was called 'infantile paralysis,' although it struck Roosevelt at the age of 40. The disease crippled Roosevelt's legs, but he eventually went on to become president of the USA.

▶ COWPOX
Once the value of Jenner's discovery became widely known, people rushed to be inoculated with cowpox in order to be protected from smallpox. This cartoon from the time shows what some people feared might happen when they were injected with cowpox – cows start growing out of their bodies!

protection against an invading microbe. This works whether the microbe is a bacterium, virus or animal parasite. In a way this reflects the views of the ancient Greeks, who believed that the body could heal itself.

The immune system uses white cells in the blood, which recognize our own body cells by the pattern of proteins on their surface. When they come across invading microbes, they attack them because they do not recognize them. They produce substances called antibodies that destroy the microbes, then other white cells eat up the microbes' remains. In this way the infection is cleared up. Next time that kind of microbe gets into the body, the white cells 'remember' which antibodies they used to eliminate it last time. They produce an army of antibodies so quickly that the infection cannot become established.

Vaccination creates immunity in the same way. The vaccine contains microbes that produce only a mild version of a disease. It usually contains dead microbes or even just parts of the microbes. This is enough for the body to mount an attack and produce antibodies. These give protection later if they are exposed to more dangerous forms of the microbe, so long as these are the same type of microbe used in the vaccine.

▶ SINGLE-DOSE SYRINGE
Modern syringes are disposable, to reduce the risk of infection. They come ready-filled with vaccine.

▶ FIRING A VACCINE
For mass vaccination, a gun was sometimes used. It fired the vaccine through each recipient's skin under very high pressure, without using a needle. These guns have now been replaced with single-dose disposable syringes.

▼ QUEUING FOR JABS
Vaccination is especially important in developing countries where there is little access to healthcare. Charities and governments carry out vaccination schedules against many killer diseases.

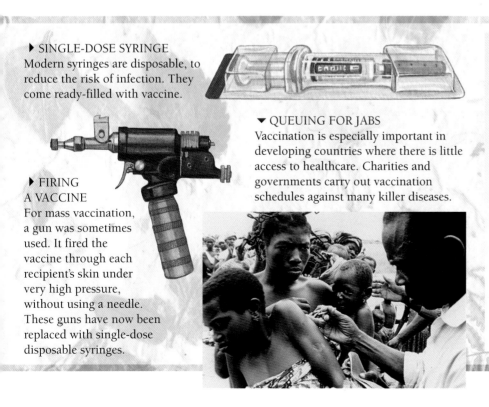

Key Dates

- 1717 Lady Wortley Montagu reports on the traditional Turkish practice of inoculation to prevent smallpox.

- 1796 Edward Jenner inoculates a boy with cowpox and demonstrates that he is then immune to smallpox.

- 1885 Pasteur tests his rabies vaccine.

- 1955 Jonas Salk's polio vaccine is introduced.

- 1979 The World Health Organization certifies that smallpox has been eradicated.

Germ Killers

Howard Florey

▲ ▼ PRIZE SCIENTISTS
Howard Florey and Ernst Chain researched penicillin together. They developed a way to mass produce this life-saving drug, and were awarded the Nobel Prize.

Ernst Chain

WHILE VACCINATION COULD PREVENT many diseases, very few infections were treatable. The first was malaria, which could be treated with quinine, extracted from the bark of the South American cinchona tree. Mercury was used to treat syphilis but proved very toxic (poisonous). A new and synthetic (manufactured) treatment called Salvarsan was introduced by Paul Ehrlich in 1910. Then in 1932 the German scientist Gerhard Domagk produced Prontosil, a red dye that attacked the streptococcus bacterium that caused many infections, such as meningitis.

A range of antibacterial drugs was developed from Prontosil. They are known as sulphonamides and prevent the multiplication of bacteria. This gives the body's immune system time to create antibodies to destroy the bacteria. Sulphonamides were not always effective, however, and sometimes caused unpleasant side effects. Also, they were completely inactive against some types of bacteria. The search for new drugs continued.

Alexander Fleming was a researcher studying the natural antibacterial substances that are produced by the body. He was particularly interested in lysozyme, a substance that is found in tears.

▼ ALEXANDER FLEMING
Fleming's discovery of penicillin was a lucky accident, but he did not realize the importance of his discovery. It was another ten years before Florey and Chain found a way to produce large quantities of penicillin.

LIFE SAVERS
Antibiotics have been used to treat all sorts of infections. They are also given to livestock and poultry to prevent disease and to make them grow quickly. As a result of being exposed to antibiotics over long periods, some bacteria have evolved methods of avoiding their effects. Nowadays, doctors try not to prescribe antibiotics for minor infections, such as sore throats, so that bacteria cannot get used to them.

◀ ANTIBIOTICS
Most antibiotics are given in the form of a powder, inside gelatine capsules, that are swallowed. However, some antibiotics are damaged by digestive juices so these have to be injected.

▼ ANTIBIOTIC ATTACK
Antibiotics work by damaging the cell wall of a bacterium.

◀ WORLD WAR II
When war broke out, the UK and US governments realized that there would soon be many wounded soldiers at risk of infection. They invested lots of money in finding a way to produce enough penicillin.

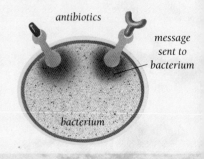

antibiotics

message sent to bacterium

bacterium

▶ PAUL EHRLICH
In the early 1900s Ehrlich produced and tested more than 600 new arsenic compounds, in an attempt for find a cure for syphilis. One of these substances, later named Salvarsan, proved very effective. It was the first drug to have a specific antibacterial effect.

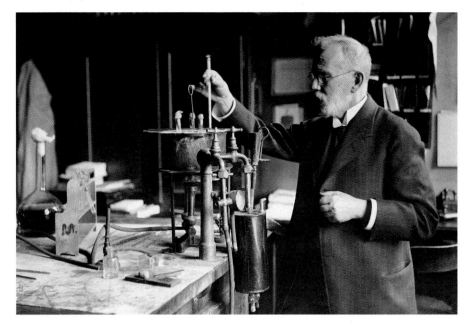

Lysozyme protects the delicate surface of the eye from bacterial attack. Fleming had also been working with staphylococci, the bacteria that cause boils. He grew colonies of these bacteria on plates of agar jelly. Returning from holiday in 1928, he noticed that a mould was growing on a discarded plate, and that the colonies of staphylococci that should have been growing around the mould had died off. Fleming identified the mould and discovered that it produced an antibiotic, called penicillin. He did not realize the importance of penicillin at the time, but, ten years later, researchers in Oxford found Fleming's report. They carried out lots of tests and found penicillin to be amazingly effective against bacteria.

The new drug proved so successful that there was a huge and immediate demand. After a huge effort, two scientists called Howard Florey and Ernst Chain found a way to produce large quantities of the mould. The drug was used during World War II to treat battle wounds. The only problem with it was that it did not kill every type of bacterium.

The worldwide search for natural organisms that will produce new antibiotics continues to this day, with deep-sea missions and journeys into tropical rainforests. When researchers find a natural antibiotic, they work out what the active parts of it are, so they can recreate this ingredient synthetically.

Most antibiotics work by stopping the bacteria from being able to build proper cell walls when they divide. Without complete cell walls, the bacteria die. Antibiotics do not usually damage human cells, because they do not have a rigid cell wall.

▲ SELMAN WAKSMAN
This American scientist invented the word 'antibiotic' in 1941. After the discovery of penicillin, Waksman looked for more antibiotics in soil microbes. In 1943 he found streptomycin, the first drug to treat TB. He received a Nobel Prize for his work.

▼ ANIMAL FEED AND ANTIBIOTICS
Antibiotics are often added to animal feed to make them grow bigger and stop them from catching disease. However, this practice has proved to be a medical disaster, because it encouraged the appearance of bacteria that could resist the effects of antibiotics. As a result, some antibiotics are now almost useless.

Key Dates

- 1910 Salvarsan is discovered by Paul Ehrlich.

- 1928 Alexander Fleming discovers penicillin by accident.

- 1935 Gerhard Domagk develops Prontosil.

- 1939 Howard Florey and Ernst Chain find a way to mass produce penicillin.

- 1943 Selman Waksman discovers streptomycin, the first drug to successfully treat TB.

- 1945 Fleming, Florey and Chain are jointly awarded the Nobel Prize for their discovery of penicillin.

Women Pioneers

WOMEN HAVE ALWAYS played a role in medicine, although right through history as late as the 1950s they were often dismissed by male doctors. Childbirth was an event from which men were usually excluded. Midwives looked after pregnant women and sometimes got rid of unwanted pregnancies. Midwives passed down their knowledge from mother to daughter, with the result that

there is little written evidence of their work. Doctors rarely recognized the importance of midwives, although a few wrote about their techniques.

There were several famous women healers during the Middle Ages. One of these, called Trotula, worked in Salerno in the 1000s. She wrote a book called *On the sufferings of women* which was used as a medical text for the next 700 years. She gave detailed instructions on the technique of diagnosis, and also published works on the diseases of children and on skin diseases.

▲ FLORENCE NIGHTINGALE
Grateful soldiers in the Crimean War nicknamed Florence Nightingale the 'Lady with the Lamp.' In the 1850s Nightingale pioneered hygienic nursing techniques.

▶ SCUTARI HOSPITAL
Florence Nightingale and her team of nurses brought in strict nursing practices. Before their arrival the field hospital at Scutari (modern-day Usküdar, in Turkey) had a very high death rate. Nightingale used her experiences to improve nursing standards when she returned to England.

STRUGGLING TO SUCCEED

Women were not usually allowed to train as doctors. They were opposed by the Church, and by male doctors too. It was not until 1849 that a woman called Elizabeth Blackwell became the first graduate doctor. In the early 1900s, suffragettes (women's rights activists) inspired many women. Marie Stopes in Britain and Margaret Sanger in the USA championed birth control. This freed women from having very large families and improved the health of women and children.

◀ DRESSING-UP
Mary Walker was an assistant surgeon in the American Civil War (1861–5). Her solution to men's distrust of female medics was to disguise herself as a man.

▶ MARIE CURIE
Women were excluded from all areas of science, not just medicine. An exception was Polish-born Marie Curie. With her French husband, Pierre, she discovered radium in 1898. Thanks to their investigations into radioactive materials, a revolutionary treatment for cancer was discovered.

▲ ELIZABETH BLACKWELL
Many medical schools turned down Blackwell before she finally qualified as a doctor in the USA in 1849. The idea of a woman doctor scandalized the medical profession. It was many years before Blackwell was fully accepted.

▶ MILITARY NURSES
By World War II (1939–45), the armed forces had a well-developed system for providing nursing care to the wounded. Mobile field hospitals and ambulance services were established. These were staffed mainly by women, who were thought too delicate for combat duties.

Hildegard was a German healer who lived at around the same time as Trotula. She combined religious and medical writing, together with natural history. In particular, she provided detailed descriptions of herbal remedies and other treatments, and was greatly respected by kings and popes.

In hospitals of the Middle Ages and the Renaissance, most nursing was carried out by nuns and other women attached to religious orders. When large hospitals were built in the 1800s, nuns played a less important role. Instead, working-class women were recruited, but they were not given any training, so the standard of nursing was poor.

The first non-religious school for nurses was set up in 1842 in Germany. Students took a three-year course, followed by exams. A woman called Florence Nightingale briefly attended this school in 1851. She completed her training in Paris and then became head of the nurses at King's College Hospital.

In 1854 Florence Nightingale was sent out to nurse the troops during the Crimean War (1853–6). Conditions in the field hospital were very bad, but by improving the hygiene in the hospitals Nightingale lowered the death rate from 40 percent to 2 percent. After the war, she opened a school of nursing at St Thomas' Hospital, London.

It took a long time, and the hard work of many brave pioneers, to change attitudes towards women in the medical profession. One such pioneer was Dr Elizabeth Blackwell. In 1869, Blackwell returned to England from the USA where she had trained in New York, despite opposition from her fellow students. She helped to found the London School of Medicine for Women. Even so, medicine remained a male dominated profession right up to the 1950s.

▲ MARGARET SANGER
A pioneer of birth control in the USA, Margaret Sanger was a nurse working mainly in slum areas. She was sent to prison for a month after opening the USA's first birth control clinic in 1916.

▼ MARIE STOPES
In 1921 Marie Stopes opened Britain's first birth control clinic, offering free consultations and contraceptives. She recommended planned families. This meant that parents would be able to limit the number of children that they had.

Key Dates

- 1849 Elizabeth Blackwell qualifies as a doctor in the USA.

- 1854 Florence Nightingale arrives at Scutari field hospital.

- 1857 Elizabeth Blackwell opens the New York Infirmary, staffed entirely by women.

- 1898 Marie Curie discovers the radioactive element radium.

- 1911 Marie Curie receives a second Nobel Prize for her work.

- 1916 Margaret Sanger opens the first birth control clinic in the USA.

- 1921 Marie Stopes opens the first birth control clinic in Britain.

Rebuilding the Body

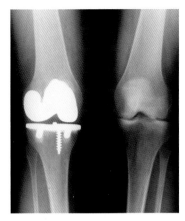

▲ ARTIFICIAL JOINTS
Many of the body's joints wear out in later life, often due to arthritis. This x-ray shows a replacement knee joint, made of metal and plastic. Many other joints can be replaced in the same way.

Prostheses are artificial body parts. False teeth are a type of prosthesis. They have been around for thousands of years, but thanks to modern plastics they are now hard to tell from the real thing.

Prostheses made huge advances during the 1900s. Artificial limbs became much lighter and looked more realistic. They can now be connected to the nervous system, so they can move like real body parts.

When limbs are broken, splints and plasters are applied

▶ HEART TRANSPLANT
Surgery to replace the heart is long and complicated. It depends on having a suitable transplant heart available. This has to be taken from a donor who has died in an accident, and must match the tissues of the recipient.

to hold them in position until the bone heals. If bones are badly shattered, metal plates are screwed onto the bone to them to give extra support. Sometimes the bone is replaced with a material such as coral. New bone cells grow into the coral, replacing it with living bone.

Heart valves damaged by disease can be replaced with mechanical ones. If the heart's natural pacemaker (that produces the heart's regular beat) is faulty, a small artificial one can be fitted. This device produces regular tiny pulses of electricity that force the heart to beat.

Transplants are another way to rebuild the body. Skin grafts are one type of transplant and blood

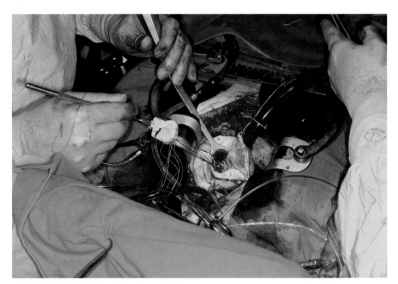

EARLY DAYS
The first example of a prosthesis was probably a tree branch. This would have been used as a simple crutch by a person with a broken leg. When surgery was developed, amputation of limbs was a common operation, though many patients died of infection. Survivors were fitted with wooden replacement limbs and hands. Sometimes simple metal hooks were used instead of hands.

◀ ROMAN FALSE TEETH
We know that false teeth were used as long ago as ancient Egyptian times. The Romans made complex gold bridges that held false teeth made from metal or ivory. Roman dentists also had various recipes for toothpastes to keep the teeth healthy.

▲ NOSE GRAFT
In the 1700s Western doctors were amazed to find that Indian surgeons were carrying out complex reconstructive surgery. This severed nose was rebuilt and then skin was grafted on. Westerners soon copied these methods for themselves.

▼ WOODEN LEGS
This pirate was unlucky enough to lose a leg and an arm. With a wooden leg and a hook for a hand, he could get about for himself. However, modern artificial limbs are far more realistic and comfortable. They have working joints and are made of lightweight plastic.

▲ ARTIFICIAL HEART VALVE
Leaking heart valves can cause ill health or death, so they are often replaced with artificial substitutes. These are simple one-way valves made from metal and plastic that will not be attacked by the immune system. Sometimes specially treated pig's heart valves are transplanted.

transfusion is another. It was tried back in the 1600s, but only became safe with more knowledge of blood groups in the 1800s.

Transplants from another person are difficult, because the immune system immediately attacks any 'foreign' organ. Very powerful drugs are needed to prevent rejection. This is why in blood transfusion the blood group of the donor (giver) has to match the recipient's (receiver's). Another problem is finding available organs. Everyone has two kidneys and lungs, and so sometimes a donor will offer one of theirs to help a sick person. Other organs, such as the liver and heart, must be removed from a healthy person who has died in an accident, so there is always a shortage of them. The first human heart transplant took place in 1967. Since then, thousands of people have received donor hearts. Most survive for a long time, but they need to take anti-rejection drugs for the rest of their lives.

Current research is looking at ways to grow complete new organs from a patient's own tissues, so they would not be rejected, though this procedure is still years away from use in human beings. Another controversial possibility is xenotransplantation, using organs from animals such as pigs.

Washable, lifelike plastic sleeve covers the arm.

Beneath the plastic, a moveable metal 'frame' forms the hand.

▶ PROSTHETIC ARM
Artificial arms can provide limited movement. Hooks or fingers are connected to the remaining arm muscles. New research is aimed at restoring more natural movement by making connections to the nerves in the arm.

▶ KIDNEY MACHINE
The only treatments for kidney failure are a new kidney transplant or regular dialysis (purifying the blood) by a kidney machine. Dialysis was first attempted with dogs in 1914, and with humans thirty years later.

▲ BLOOD GROUPS
Karl Landsteiner identified blood groups in 1901–2. He called the blood types O, A, B and AB. This made it possible to give patients blood from donors who match their own group.

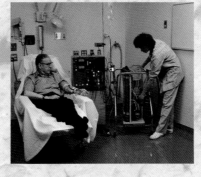

◀ TREATING DIABETES
In 1921, Charles Best and Frederick Banting saved the life of a diabetic dog with insulin taken from another animal's pancreas. This led to the modern use of artifically produced insulin to treat diabetes.

Charles Best   Frederick Banting

Key Dates

- 2500BC Egyptians use false teeth.
- 1901–2 Karl Landsteiner describes blood groups, making blood transfusion a practical possibility.
- 1921 Banting and Best use insulin to treat diabetes in dogs.
- 1950s Synthetic insulin is produced.
- 1954 First successful kidney transplant.
- 1960 First pacemaker is fitted.
- 1960s Artificial hips and other joints are introduced.
- 1963 First lung transplant.
- 1967 Christiaan Barnard performs the first human heart transplant.

Healing the Mind

AFTER THEY had been neglected for centuries, hospitals for the insane were eventually developed in the 1400s, mostly to keep the inmates away from the rest of society. The Bethlehem Royal Hospital in London was among the earliest of the asylums, taking live-in patients from 1403. The inmates were kept in terrible conditions. Most were chained up, and visitors were encouraged to come and view the patients as a form of entertainment. This was common throughout Europe.

The first real advance came around 1800. Philippe Pinel, a Parisian psychiatrist (doctor for the mentally ill), abolished the practice of chaining up the patients in the Bicêtre asylum for men and Salpêtrière asylum for women. Pinel's pupil, Esquirol, came up with the idea of a community where patients lived together with their

▲ STRAITJACKET
Before there were drugs to calm violent patients, straitjackets were used to restrain them.

▶ THE MADHOUSE
In its early years, the Bethlehem Hospital, known as Bedlam, was a place full of suffering. Patients were often kept chained up and even beaten.

MODERN FORMS OF THERAPY
Psychotherapy marked a departure from traditional ideas about the cause and treatment of mental illness. Psychiatrists began to look closely at the emotional problems that seem to cause mental illness and to explore these with their patients in order to give them an insight into their condition.

▶ ECT
Electroconvulsive therapy (ECT) was widely used in the 1950s and 1960s to treat severe depression. Doctors pass a powerful current through the brain, causing a convulsion and, sometimes, relief of depression. It can also cause memory loss, however, so ECT is now only used as a last resort.

▲ ART THERAPY
Modern psychiatric clinics encourage patients to express themselves through painting. This is especially helpful to patients who bottle up their emotions because they are unable to speak freely about how they feel.

▼ PSYCHIATRIST'S CHAIR
It is very important, when a patient is being examined by a psychiatrist, that they are relaxed. This is why many psychiatrists will have comfortable chairs, like this one, or even couches, for their patients.

doctors in a group. Instead of being treated as crazed brutes, patients were seen as individuals who could be helped. This treatment sometimes improved their condition enough for them to be discharged (let out) into society.

Not all treatment became humane. Many famous psychiatrists still chained up their patients, beat them, or plunged them into cold baths in a form of shock treatment. However, living conditions in most asylums improved greatly.

In the mid-1800s Charcot, another physician at the Salpêtrière hospital, made a unique study of the patients in his care. He described their condition in great detail, and also studied hypnosis as a form of treatment. Then, at the end of the 1800s, the German doctor Emil Kraepelin began to classify the most serious mental illnesses. He was the first to accurately describe schizophrenia.

From the 1880s, Sigmund Freud developed psychoanalysis, which

▲ FREEING THE INSANE
Philippe Pinel was the first doctor to introduce humane treatment of the insane. He ordered the chains and restraints to be removed from patients in the French hospitals where he worked.

▶ SIGMUND FREUD
Freud's great innovation was to try to understand what caused mental illness. He encouraged his patients to talk about their past experiences. This is a very long, drawn-out process. It is not as practical as drugs for treating large numbers of people.

attempted to show how a patient's problems were the result of previous experiences. Carl Jung developed Freud's ideas further. Some Freudian and Jungian methods of exploring a patient's history are still used today.

The other big development during the 1900s was the use of drugs. Once it was known that there are chemical changes in the brains of the mentally ill, drugs were designed to help the brain chemistry become normal again. However, drugs brought a new set of problems, including addiction, and so the search for a perfect solution continues.

▲ WHAT MIGHT THIS BE?
The Swiss psychiatrist Hermann Rorschach came up with his inkblot test in 1918. He asked the patient what the spilt ink looked like. Their answers might give a clue as to what was worrying them.

▼ CHEMICAL TREATMENT
Prozac is one of a class of new drugs that is intended to restore the balance of brain chemicals. Scientists try to find drugs that restore normal mental health without causing serious side effects. Drugs are used to treat people suffering from depression, schizophrenia and other psychiatric problems.

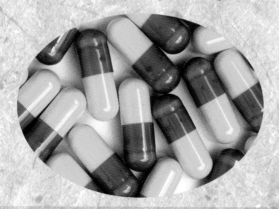

Key Dates

- 1377 Bethlehem Hospital begins to admit insane patients.

- 1793 Philippe Pinel frees the insane from their chains.

- 1856–1939 Life of Sigmund Freud, pioneer of psychoanalysis.

- 1943 The accidental discovery of LSD stimulates scientific interest in the effect of drugs on the brain. This leads to the production of drugs to treat conditions such as anxiety and schizophrenia.

- 1950s–60s ECT is widely used to treat severe depression.

- 1990s Prozac and related drugs are used to treat depression.

Plants and Pills

ERBS HAVE BEEN used by people to treat disease since prehistoric times. They have been found in some of the most ancient tombs and burials. Some herbs were used because of their obvious benefits, while others were used for magical or spiritual reasons. The belief that the appearance of a plant revealed its possible use as a medicine was known as the doctrine of signatures.

It is said that 80 per cent of the world's population still depends upon herbal medicine, though only a few herbal remedies form part of conventional Western medicine. Many of those used today are the same as those mentioned in ancient records of the Egyptians.

▲ DIGITALIS
Foxglove contains the drug digitalis, which is still used for the treatment of heart failure.

▶ APOTHECARY
The medieval apothecary diagnosed illness and carried out treatments, as well as making herbal remedies and other drugs.

ADMINISTERING DRUGS

Most drugs are given by mouth in the form of tablets or medicine, but they come in many other forms. Lung diseases can be treated by breathing in a finely powdered drug, straight into the lungs. Injection is used to give large amounts of a drug very quickly, or to give a drug that would be damaged by the digestive system. Some drugs given by injection are in a form that is absorbed only very slowly into the tissues, so they have a prolonged effect.

▼ DRUG MANUFACTURING
Modern drugs companies use high-tech production lines to prepare medicines on a large scale. The process needs to be checked at every stage to ensure the quality of the drugs.

▲ SLOW-RELEASE CAPSULES
Some drugs disappear from the body very rapidly. People would have to take many doses throughout the day to keep enough of the drug in the bloodstream. Slow-release capsules let the drug out very gradually, so patients only need to take one or two capsules each day.

The herbal preparations described by Galen and other Greek doctors were preserved by Arab scribes. They continued to be used in the Middle Ages. Many monasteries and apothecaries grew herb gardens. Renaissance explorers brought back new herbs from freshly discovered lands. The herbal written by Nicholas Culpeper in 1649, titled *A Physicall Directory*, contains a wealth of detailed observation, and remains in print today.

Over the years, many of the plants listed in the old herbals fell out of fashion, but some of the most effective remedies are still used. Cinchona bark contains quinine and was introduced into Western medicine in the 1600s as a cure for malaria. Foxglove was used from 1785 to treat dropsy and doctors slowly saw that this was a valuable treatment for certain types of heart disease.

Many herbs were extremely poisonous unless they were carefully prepared. For example, colchicine, extracted from the crocus flower, can be lethal, but is a good treatment for gout. The extraction of the active part of herbal remedies soon became a science, after alchemists discovered the technique of distillation. This involved boiling up a liquid so that the water evaporated (turned into steam), leaving behind a concentrated essence.

These techniques of purification led to the founding of the modern pharmaceutical (drugs) industry. Many modern drugs are synthetic, or artificially manufactured, versions of plant extracts. There are continuing worldwide searches to identify traditional remedies and to investigate their active ingredients.

◀ THE GARDEN OF HEALTH
The Hortus Sanitatis *(Garden of Health) is a typical herbal written in Germany in the 1400s. It lists the drugs used by apothecaries and the properties the drugs were believed to have. Most of the information comes from the time of Hippocrates.*

◀ WILLOW BARK
Extracts of willow bark have traditionally been used as a painkiller, but it was not until 1852 that a version of the active drug was made synthetically. It was soon marketed as aspirin.

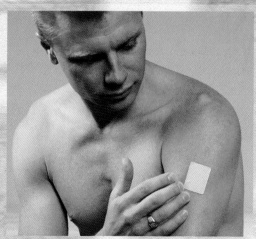

▲ NICOTINE PATCH
Some drugs can be absorbed through the skin. The nicotine patch allows small amounts of nicotine to flow into the bloodstream, helping smokers overcome their addiction to cigarettes.

▼ INHALER
Drugs for asthma are usually delivered straight into the lungs, by means of an inhaler. These drugs are sometimes in the form of a very fine powder. This puts the drug where it needs to be to work, and reduces any side effects elsewhere in the body.

Key Dates

- 1852 Aspirin is first synthesized.

- 1903 Barbiturate sedative (calming) drugs are introduced. They contain barbituric acid naturally found in the lichen *Usnea barbata*.

- 1930s Cortisone is isolated, leading to the development of modern steroid drugs.

- 1935 Sulphonamide antibacterial drugs are developed.

- 1961 The sedative thalidomide is withdrawn after causing terrible damage to unborn babies.

- 1980s AZT is developed as a treatment for AIDS sufferers.

Alternative Therapies

SOME PEOPLE TOTALLY reject modern medicine. Christian Scientists, for example, believe that prayer and faith can cure all disease. Jehovah's Witnesses reject only some aspects of conventional medicine, such as transfusions.

Not all people reject traditional treatment for religious reasons. Some people find that their condition cannot be cured by orthodox (traditional) medicine, so look for an alternative. Also, while many people still respect a doctor's advice so much that they would never dream of questioning it, others may be sufficiently well-informed about their illness to wish to take treatment into their own hands.

In the 1990s there was increased interest in alternatives to traditional medicine. There is a difference between alternative therapies, in which a person rejects conventional medicine and seeks some other form of therapy, and complementary medicine, in which patients take extra steps as well as the treatment prescribed by their doctor. Most doctors accept

▲ CAMOMILE
Extracts of camomile are widely used for pain relief in homeopathic medicine. Homeopaths use tiny quantities of drugs that produce similar symptoms to those of the condition they wish to treat.

▶ MOXIBUSTION
One type of acupuncture is moxibustion, in which cones of herbs are burned on the skin at points on some of the meridians (channels) described by Chinese medicine.

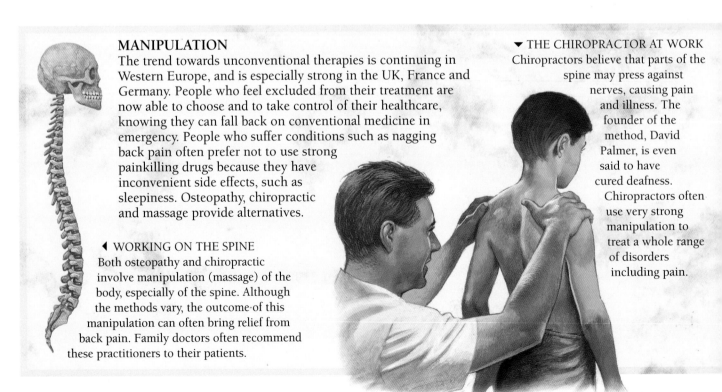

MANIPULATION
The trend towards unconventional therapies is continuing in Western Europe, and is especially strong in the UK, France and Germany. People who feel excluded from their treatment are now able to choose and to take control of their healthcare, knowing they can fall back on conventional medicine in emergency. People who suffer conditions such as nagging back pain often prefer not to use strong painkilling drugs because they have inconvenient side effects, such as sleepiness. Osteopathy, chiropractic and massage provide alternatives.

◀ WORKING ON THE SPINE
Both osteopathy and chiropractic involve manipulation (massage) of the body, especially of the spine. Although the methods vary, the outcome of this manipulation can often bring relief from back pain. Family doctors often recommend these practitioners to their patients.

▼ THE CHIROPRACTOR AT WORK
Chiropractors believe that parts of the spine may press against nerves, causing pain and illness. The founder of the method, David Palmer, is even said to have cured deafness. Chiropractors often use very strong manipulation to treat a whole range of disorders including pain.

that their patients may use complementary therapies and do not mind as long as these do not interfere with conventional treatments. In Britain, 40 percent of family doctors routinely refer patients to complementary therapists. Alternative therapies, though, can mean that a sick person delays going to their doctor and this can make their problem much more difficult to treat.

Some of these therapies are difficult to define. Herbal treatments, for example, can be a form of conventional medicine if they are known to contain medically active ingredients. Where their effectiveness is not proven, they are classed as alternative or complementary therapies.

Acupuncture is an ancient Chinese healing technique where needles are inserted into the body. Science dismissed this technique as quackery until, in recent years, it was found that acupuncture at certain points has a powerful painkilling effect. Acupuncture is especially helpful for lingering pains that do not respond to drugs.

What is common to all forms of complementary and alternative medicine is that they have no scientific explanation. Some believe that they work because of the placebo (inactive drug) effect. Placebos given to patients in medical trials often work as well as the real drugs, probably because the patient really believes that they will.

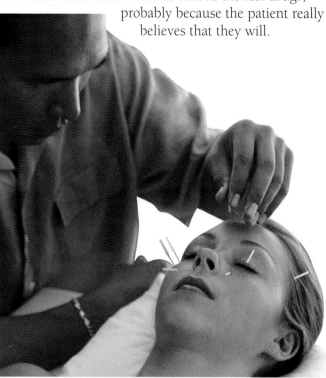

▶ AROMATHERAPY
Smells have a powerful effect on the body and on mood. Aromatherapy depends on massaging the body with scented oils, or on breathing in the fumes of heated oils. This helps the patient to relax and may have an effect on some illnesses.

▲ ACUPUNCTURE
Scientific research has shown that acupuncture, the Chinese practice of inserting needles into the skin, really does kill pain. Serious operations have been performed in China with no other form of painkiller except acupuncture.

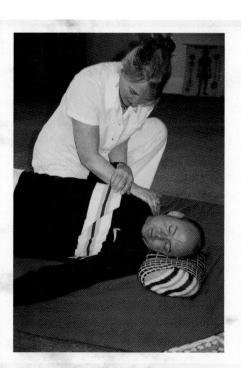

◀ SHIATSU
This is a technique to relieve pain that evolved in Japan during the 1900s. Practitioners of shiatsu use their fingers to press hard on acupuncture points, and also use massage and meditation to treat their patients.

▶ FEET FIRST
Reflexology is based on the idea that different areas on the feet represent different parts of the body. Massage and stimulation of these areas can help treat illness and generally improve health.

Key Dates

- 300BC First descriptions of acupuncture in the *Nei Ching*.

- AD1601 Acupuncture discussed in detail by Yang Chi-chou.

- 1796 Samuel Hahnemann says that 'like cures like' and develops homeopathy in Germany.

- 1874 American doctor Andrew Still introduces osteopathy.

- 1895 Chiropractic is developed in the USA by David Palmer.

- 1900s Shiatsu is developed.

- 1930s Reflexology is introduced by Eunice Ingham.

Holistic Medicine

▲ NO SMOKING
Holistic medicine points out the need to avoid activities that have health risks, such as smoking.

THE OLDEST FORMS of medicine are enjoying a comeback. Modern holistic medicine is an approach that treats the whole patient, not just the disease. It is a way to maintain good health rather than cure illness. The most important influences on today's holistic medicine are ancient Chinese medicine and Indian Ayurvedic medicine, both of which promoted whole body health.

Holistic medicine usually combines diet, physical exercise and meditation, together with other alternative techniques such as aromatherapy, reflexology and acupuncture. Herbal treatment is influenced by the writings of Culpeper as well as Chinese and Ayurvedic medicine. Homeopathy is one of the forms of holistic medicine which is widely used in Europe and the USA.

Homeopathy began in Germany in the early 1800s, when Samuel Hahnemann described how very tiny doses of a drug had an effect on his patients. According to Hahnemann, the more the drug was diluted, the stronger its effects. The substance selected would produce similar effects to the disease itself if given in large doses. In the UK homeopathy is regarded as an unconventional but just about acceptable therapy.

Meditation and contemplation have an important role in holistic therapy. They were brought to Europe by Indian teachers who combined Ayurvedic medicine with Western beliefs. Transcendental meditation is one

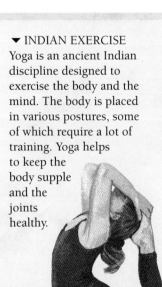

◀ HEALTHY FOOD
There is growing awareness of what a healthy diet must contain and how this improves health. Most people know that they should cut down on junk foods, and especially sugar, salt and fats, if they want to reduce the risk of health problems later in life. Fresh fruit and vegetables are an important part of a healthy diet. They contain vitamins that supply the body with essential minerals.

DEALING WITH STRESS
Stress is an inescapable part of modern living. It can lead to illnesses such as high blood pressure and ulcers and to emotional problems such as panic attacks and depression. The conventional solution is to take drugs for these conditions. The holistic approach is to relieve stress by relaxation techniques such as yoga, t'ai chi and meditation.

◀ EASTERN ART
T'ai chi is an ancient martial art that was developed in China in the 1700s. It uses the principles of *yin* and *yang* to balance body and mind in slow-motion exercises.

▼ INDIAN EXERCISE
Yoga is an ancient Indian discipline designed to exercise the body and the mind. The body is placed in various postures, some of which require a lot of training. Yoga helps to keep the body supple and the joints healthy.

▲ YOGIC MEDITATION
This yogi is meditating in a form of the lotus position, known as the half-lotus. Yogic meditation was made popular in the West by Indian mystics such as the Maharishi Mahesh Yogi and his movement for Transcendental Meditation.

◄ KEEPING FIT
Exercise is an important part of holistic therapy. It is used to burn up excess body fat, and build up muscle. Another very important benefit is that exercise is fun. Feeling happy has been shown to have a good effect on people's health.

▼ LIFE ON THE STOCK EXCHANGE
Modern business life means constant stress and this can eventually produce changes in the body that cause illnesses such as anxiety, depression and ulcers. Many holistic techniques try to work against this stress.

of the best known of these techniques. People repeat a mantra (chant) inside their head to reach a state of deep relaxation.

The holistic movement has made many conventional doctors look at the whole patient, not just the disease. Lifestyle, emotional problems and diet are just some of the factors that can affect a person's health. Holistic therapy emphasizes good diet, exercise and fresh air, all of which contribute to health. Some clinics now offer holistic therapy along with traditional treatments, so that their patients can choose a combination of therapies that suits them. One problem with holistic therapy is that it is difficult for a people to be sure a therapist is reputable. To solve this, many countries want alternative therapists to form professional bodies.

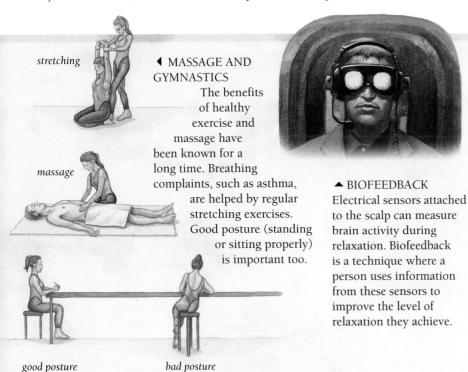

stretching

massage

good posture   *bad posture*

◄ MASSAGE AND GYMNASTICS
The benefits of healthy exercise and massage have been known for a long time. Breathing complaints, such as asthma, are helped by regular stretching exercises. Good posture (standing or sitting properly) is important too.

▲ BIOFEEDBACK
Electrical sensors attached to the scalp can measure brain activity during relaxation. Biofeedback is a technique where a person uses information from these sensors to improve the level of relaxation they achieve.

Key Dates

- 200BC Zuang Zi describes the importance of maintaining balance of *ch'i* (vital energy or breath) in the body.

- 200BC Yoga develops in India.

- AD1700s T'ai chi develops in China.

- 1959 Maharishi Mahesh Yogi's first world tour brings Transcendental Meditation to the West.

- 1968 Aerobic exercise is developed by Kenneth Cooper.

- 1980s Biofeedback is developed as an aid to relaxation.

Modern Technology

Since the 1960s medical technology has advanced faster than earlier doctors could ever have dreamed. For example, the laser, which produces a thin beam of intense light, was created. It can be used as a scalpel to cut through tissue painlessly. The laser beam can be moved very precisely, which means it can be used to remove cancers and to perform delicate surgery on the eye or even inside the brain, without any damage to healthy tissues.

▲ LASER SCALPEL
The intense beam of light produced by a laser can be used for very precise surgery. As it burns through tissue it seals the wound. Lasers are often used in skin surgery to remove birthmarks and tattoos.

▶ KEYHOLE SURGERY
Some modern operations are carried out through a tiny hole made in the patient's body. A small probe is fed through the hole. This sends a picture of the inside of the patient to a large screen, so that the surgeon can see what he or she is doing.

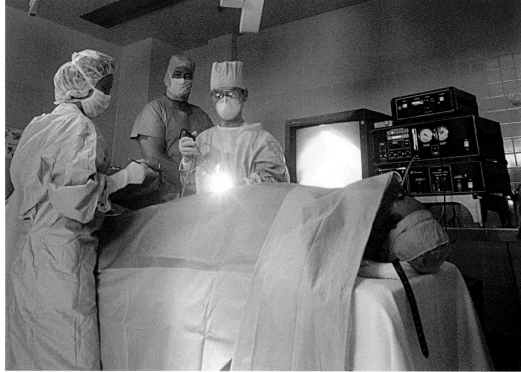

LATEST TECHNIQUES

Technological advances are constantly being made, along with more effective drugs. Sometimes simple devices can transform the life of a sick person, such as a tiny tube inserted into a blocked blood vessel to keep it open. Some technology, however, is extremely complex, such as the computerized monitoring equipment used in life support systems. Many modern techniques, such as keyhole surgery, have a quicker recovery time and this cuts down how long a patient has to spend in hospital.

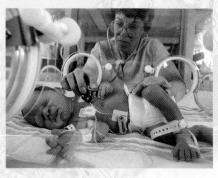

◀ THE CHANCE OF LIFE
Tiny premature babies would once have died. Today they survive in special care baby units. They breathe filtered, warm air and all their body functions are monitored. Sometimes they are given special drugs to improve their lung function.

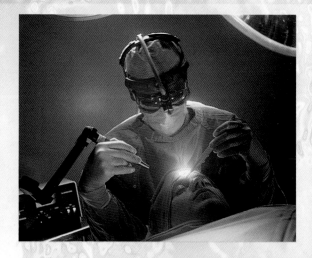

▲ HI-TECH EYE SURGERY
Lasers can be used for surgery on the eye without the need to cut open this delicate organ. The laser can fire through the pupil, burning a series of tiny spots that can weld a displaced retina into place.

Pain relief is usually achieved with the use of drugs, but sometimes other technology is used to reduce the patient's dependence on these painkillers. The success of some types of acupuncture in controlling pain led to the experiment of applying tiny electrical currents to the nerves controlling pain. The experiment worked and now TENS (transcutaneous – through the skin – electrical nerve stimulation) is a common method for the relief of chronic pain.

Patients suffering extreme pain, for example in advanced cancer, need analgesic (pain-relieving) drugs continuously. This is achieved by implanting a needle in the affected area. The drug is drip-fed using a tiny battery-powered pump worn at the waist on a belt.

Premature babies (babies born early) are always at risk because their lungs are not properly formed. The earliest technology to help these tiny babies was heated incubators that kept them warm. Today even a tiny infant weighing just one kilogram can survive in a special care baby unit. Computers monitor the amount of oxygen in the baby's blood, its body temperature and breathing. In the same way, life support systems keep people alive after devastating brain injuries that would once have killed them. People in a coma can be supported for many years, although after this time they rarely recover.

Electric shocks can kill, but the defibrillator is a device that delivers a powerful shock to the heart to restart it after a heart attack. It forms an essential part of the emergency equipment in a modern hospital.

Kidney dialysis is a method that removes wastes from the blood of people whose kidneys do not work. Normally the build up of these wastes would quickly poison them, but with dialysis several times a week they can live a relatively normal life, although a kidney transplant is their only chance of complete recovery.

▶ LIFE SUPPORT MACHINE
A life support machine can carry out many of the vital functions of the body. People who have been severely injured in an accident can be looked after by the life support machine. This allows time for their body to heal itself. Sometimes people with severe brain damage can be kept alive for many years on a life support system.

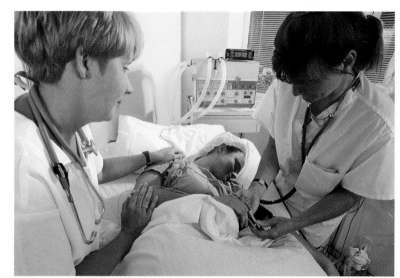

▼ BRAIN SURGERY
The brain does not have any sensory organs on its surface, so brain surgery can be carried out on a fully conscious (awake) patient. A hole is drilled in the head under local anaesthetic. This stereotactic frame allows the surgeon to position his or her instruments very precisely.

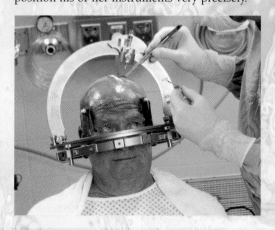

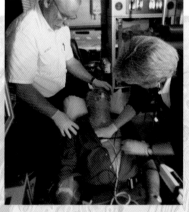

▲ TREATMENT ON THE ROAD
The original idea of an ambulance was to get a sick person to hospital as fast as possible. Today, treatment is often begun during the journey. Paramedics trained in emergency medicine save the lives of many people who may otherwise have died before reaching hospital.

Key Dates

- 1917 Albert Einstein defines the scientific principles of the laser.

- 1928 The 'iron lung' is invented to assist the breathing of people paralysed by polio. It is widely used up to the 1950s.

- 1960 The laser scalpel is invented.

- 1978 The first 'test-tube baby' is born after research by Patrick Steptoe and RG Edwards. This is opposed by the Church, but becomes widely used.

- 1985 Keyhole surgery becomes popular. Patients recover more quickly from this form of surgery.

Imaging the Body

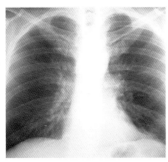

▲ CHEST X-RAY
X-rays pass more slowly through solid bone than through soft tissue. This means bones show up in an x-ray image, but flesh does not. X-rays got their name because Wilhelm Röntgen, who discovered them, did not know exactly what they were. They are now also called Röntgen rays, and as well as in medicine, they are also used for looking for defects in solid objects.

T HE ONLY WAY that early doctors could know what was going on inside their patients' bodies was to open them up, or to peer in through natural openings into the body. Stethoscopes helped to reveal the working of the heart, and soon ophthalmoscopes allowed doctors to look inside the eye. Endoscopes were developed in 1805 and worked rather like a slim telescope. They were inserted down the gullet to view the stomach lining, up the anus to examine the rectum or through the vagina to explore the condition of a woman's reproductive organs. Early endoscopes were rigid and extremely unpleasant for the patient, but in the 1930s flexible ones were introduced. These worked by fibre optics, in which a bundle of tiny flexible glass fibres was used

▼ AN EARLY X-RAY
Wilhelm Röntgen, who discovered x-rays, took the first x-ray photographs. This image shows his wife's hand. Her wedding ring is clearly visible, along with an old penny and a pair of compasses, because x-rays cannot pass through metal.

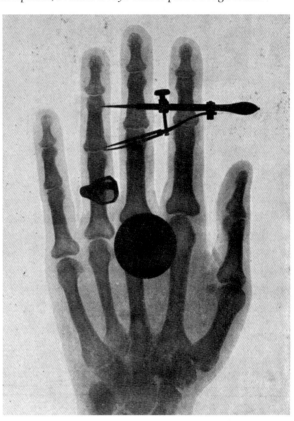

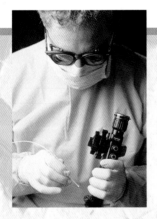

▲ ENDOSCOPE
The endoscope is a telescope-like device that is inserted into the body through a small cut. It can be moved around so that surgeon can identify a diseased area.

INSIDE VIEW
Accurate imaging of the internal parts of the body makes surgery safer and more accurate. Massive scanners are used for non-invasive investigations. The endoscope has now been refined so much that, in a procedure called a laparotomy, a tiny fibre-optic tube is inserted through a small hole in the abdomen. This allows the doctor to view the internal organs while the patient is under a local anaesthetic. Sometimes a form of keyhole surgery can be carried out with tiny instruments fitted to the same device.

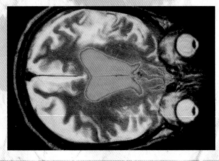

◀ SLICE OF LIFE
MRI produces a 3-D picture of the inside of the body. It uses powerful magnetic energy to photograph soft tissues that are not visible to x-rays.

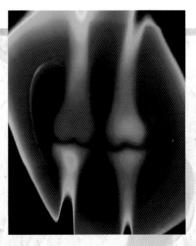

▲ HOT SPOTS
Infection or inflammation can raise the temperature of the affected part of the body. Thermal imaging cameras detect these temperature changes and produce a thermogram (heat picture), to show the doctor where the hot spots are.

to conduct an image. Modern endoscopes have been refined so that they carry their own light source and tiny instruments such as scalpels and grabs that retrieve samples of tissue. The bundle of light fibres can even take photographs inside the body.

The most important discovery to help doctors view the inside of the body was accidental. In 1895 the German scientist Wilhelm Röntgen discovered x-rays while investigating cathode rays. He received the Nobel Prize for his discovery six years later. Almost at once, people realized how useful x-rays could be for medical diagnosis. By the 1920s, x-ray clinics had become an important part of the war against tuberculosis.

A new method for imaging the inside of the body was developed in the 1950s, as a result of research during World War I. Sonar (sound navigation and ranging) used high-frequency sound waves that bounced off a submerged submarine and could be recorded at the surface. Using this technique, ultrasound could pick up echoes from soft tissues, such as cancers, that could not be readily seen on x-rays. The technique worked just as well on the foetus within the womb. Ultrasound scanning is now a routine procedure during pregnancy.

X-rays and ultrasound scans produce a simple image, but in 1967, Godfrey Hounsfield hit on the idea of producing sections through the body that could be put together by a computer to create a 3-D image. This resulted in the development of the CAT (computerized axial tomography) scanner in which patients are placed in a huge machine while the x-ray device revolves

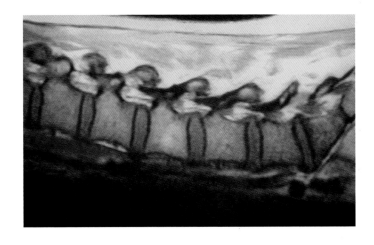

▲ CAT SCAN OF THE LOWER BACK
To produce a CAT scan, an x-ray machine is rotated about the patient's body, taking a series of pictures. Then a computer generates a scan picture that looks look a section through the complete body. CAT scans even show soft tissues that do not normally appear on x-rays.

around them, photographing slices through their bodies. A similar method is to inject the patient with a radioactive dye that shows up in the photographs taken by the scanner.

The MRI (magnetic resonance imaging) scanner is one of the most recent innovations. It is safer than other imaging techniques, because it uses magnetic energy, not harmful radiation. It can even show changes in body chemistry as they take place. For example, it can show which parts of the brain become active as we think, talk or move.

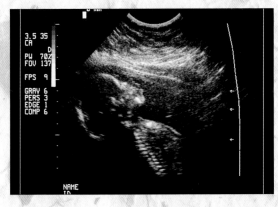

▲ UNBORN BABY
Ultrasound is used to check on the health of babies in the womb. They produce live images that even show the baby's heart beating.

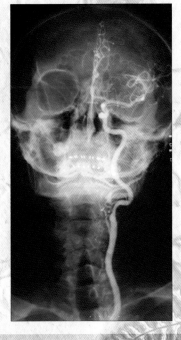

▶ ARTERIOGRAM
Damage to arterial (blood vessel) walls shows up when a dye is injected into the artery. X-rays cannot pass through this dye, and show the shape of the artery in the x-ray.

Key Dates

- 1805 AJ Desormeaux develops the first endoscope in Paris.
- 1895 German physicist Wilhelm Röntgen discovers x-rays.
- 1916 Sonar is used to detect enemy submarines in World War I.
- 1950s Ultrasound scanning is developed by Ian Donald.
- 1953 Arteriography is perfected.
- 1967 Godfrey Hounsfield develops the CAT scanner.
- 1972 The first clinical test of CAT scanning is a success.
- 1980s MRI scans are introduced.

Looking to the Future

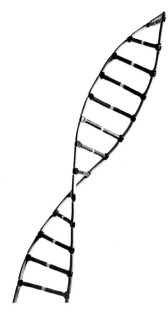

SCIENCE AND MEDICINE are still advancing at an ever-increasing rate. Modern innovations are usually the work of teams of people, each with their own special knowledge, rather than talented individuals.

One of the most important innovations has been techniques that allow us to read the genetic structure of the human cell. Before long every one of the millions of genes in every human cell will have been mapped, and the function of many of them will be understood. This is significant because many devastating diseases are caused by genetic abnormalities (accidental changes that occur in the genes as cells reproduce). These affect the function of the body and cause disease. It will be possible to identify people carrying these defective genes so they can make a decision about whether or not to risk having children. Research is already taking place into gene therapy, where corrected genes are inserted into an affected person's body. This is being tried in cystic fibrosis, an inherited lung disease. Modified genes are sprayed into the lungs of affected children to try to correct the condition.

Drugs are providing treatments for more and more diseases. New drugs are designed on computers that produce images of the molecular structure of a whole range of similar drugs. This can show researchers how to modify the molecule to produce

▲ CODE OF LIFE
DNA holds the code for the structure of the whole human body inside each living cell. Research into DNA is revealing the causes of many diseases.

▶ VIRTUAL SURGERY
Virtual reality (VR) allows students and surgeons to perform surgery without endangering a real patient.

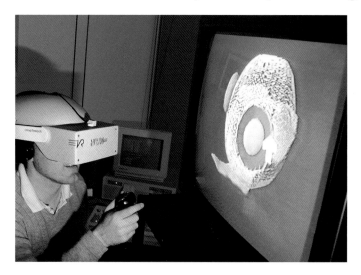

WHAT NEXT?
Medical techniques are becoming more sophisticated and, at the same time, far more expensive. Some medical innovations are so costly that there might have to be rationing if routine medical care is to continue. Already there are long waiting lists for certain operations, and the latest anti-cancer drugs are too expensive for all patients to be given these life-saving treatments.

◀ WORKING WITH THE IMMUNE SYSTEM
Immunology (studying the immune system) is a very important branch of medical science, because it makes sense to encourage the body to protect itself. At the same time, the wrong type of immune reactions can cause disease.

◀ GM FOODS
Bioengineers can already genetically modify (alter the genes of) our foods. For example, some crops now have built in resistance to insect pests. Maybe one day scientists will be able to give foods built in medicines for good health. However, some people question the safety of GM crops.

▶ BUILT TO ATTACK
Bacteriophages are forms of virus that prey on bacteria like this. Genetic engineering may be used to design bacteriophages that fight specific diseases.

effects, even before a drug has been synthesized.

Modern technology is already helping many family doctors. Sometimes, the doctor may need to refer a patient to a specialist for a detailed diagnosis. Modern teleconferencing means that, via his or her computer, the doctor can speak directly to a specialist who could even be in another country. The specialist could then examine the patient by video link.

Technology concentrates mostly on medicine in developed countries, but throughout the world, millions of people do not have access to medical care at all or, if they do, cannot afford the treatment. It is a challenge for doctors and governments around the worlds to improve the standards of health for everyone. Agencies such as the World Health Organization have made huge efforts to set up global health strategies. These are aimed at diseases that could be easily controlled by vaccination or the use of inexpensive drugs.

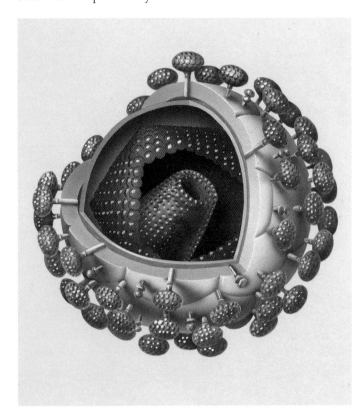

◀ HIV VIRUS
The HIV virus associated with AIDS has been studied more closely than any other virus, and its structure is well understood. What is less clear is how the virus constantly changes to avoid being attacked by the immune system. Efforts are underway to find ever more effective treatments to slow down the disease, but at present there is no vaccine or cure.

▶ SMART LOO
A diagnostic toilet has been developed in Japan. Sensors check the weight of the user and measure the fat and sugar content of their wastes. The toilet sends its results direct to the doctor.

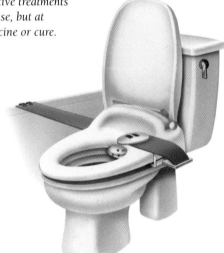

▼ ZERO GRAVITY
Research has already taken place in orbiting spacecraft to investigate new ways to purify drugs. The lack of gravity in space has profound effects on the body. It is possible that people with muscle-wasting diseases could survive longer under these conditions.

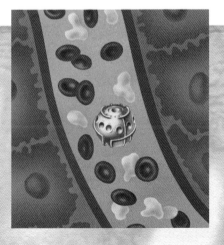

▲ NANO ROBOTS
There are plans to produce nano robots, robots small enough to travel around the body in the bloodstream. These robots could be programmed to monitor a person's health, attack cancers, or remove cholesterol (fatty build ups) from blocked arteries.

Key Dates

- 1869 DNA is discovered.

- 1943 Scientists discover that DNA passes on genetic information.

- 1953 James Watson and Francis Crick discover the double-helix structure of DNA.

- 1961 Yuri Gagarin is the first man to travel into space.

- 1970s Genetic engineering begins.

- 1980s Virtual reality is developed.

- 1990s Medical research in zero gravity begins.

- 1990 GM yeast goes on sale in the UK.

Glossary

A

acupuncture Traditional Chinese treatment, by pushing needles through the skin at specific points.

alchemy An early form of chemistry, which looked for a way to change base metals into precious ones, and for the secret of eternal life.

alternative medicine Systems of unconventional treatments, used instead of 'science-based' medicine.

amputation To cut off a damaged or diseased limb.

anaesthetic Substance that prevents feeling in all or part of the body.

anatomy The study of the structure of the body – where everything is and how it fits together.

antibiotic A drug, typically based on a natural substance, that attacks germs.

antibody A substance produced by the body's immune system, that kills or weakens microbes.

antisepsis Prevention of infection by killing microbes, using antiseptics or ultraviolet light.

apothecary An old name for a pharmacist.

Persian apothecaries mix a medicine

asepsis Prevention of infection by stopping the presence of microbes.

asylum An old term for a hospital in which the mentally ill were treated and, usually, locked away.

B

bacterium Member of a group of microbes (bacteria) that cause many common infections.

barber-surgeon A person who did the jobs of both barber and surgeon.

birth control Method of preventing pregnancy and therefore controlling the growth of the population.

C

cauterization Use of heat to seal blood vessels during surgery, once carried out with red-hot irons.

complementary medicine Systems of unconventional medicine, used as well as 'science-based' medicine.

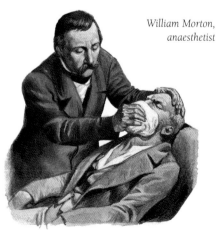

William Morton, anaesthetist

D

diagnosis Identification of a disease from its symptoms.

dissection Cutting up a body or an organ in order to see its structure.

disease Any disorder that causes illness, such as diabetes or epilepsy, with or without infection from germs.

E

epidemic A widespread outbreak of an infectious disease.

H

herbal Substance, such as a drug, made from plants. Also used to mean a book that lists herbs and their properties.

holistic medicine System of medicine that tries to maintain health by treating the whole body.

colonies of bacteria

hygiene A condition of cleanliness which helps maintain health. In medicine, hygiene means an absence of disease-producing microbes.

I

immune system Body system that defends against disease by producing antibodies.

immunity Condition in which the body has experienced and fought off a microbe attack, and has the antibodies to fight them off next time.

infection Disease caused by an invading microbe.

inoculation Introducing a microbe into the body to produce a controlled infection that will provide immunity to a disease.

M

microbe A microscopic organism, such as a bacterium, virus or fungus.

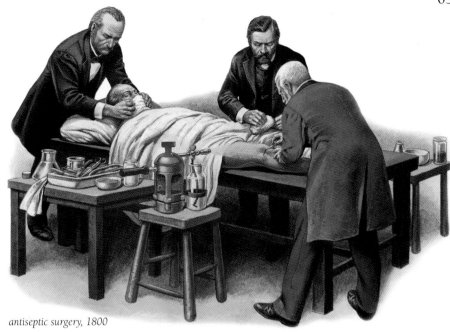

antiseptic surgery, 1800

mortality Death, or the frequency or number of deaths.

O

organism An entire living animal or plant, including its cells, organs and chemical reactions.

P

pharmacist A specialist trained in preparing and supplying drugs.

physician A doctor of medicine.

poultice An ointment that is spread on a bandage, or mixed with purified clay, and then placed on an inflamed or injured part.

prognosis The expected course or outcome of a disease.

prosthesis An artificial organ or body part, such as a heart valve, glass eye or artificial limb.

psychiatrist A doctor who studies the workings of the mind and treats mental illness.

psychotherapy Treatment of mental illness by helping a patient see the cause of his or her condition.

Q

quack Slang term for a person selling useless drugs or 'cures.'

S

sanitation Measures for hygiene, such as sewage disposal.

surgeon A doctor who operates on diseased or injured organs.

T

therapy Non-surgical treatment.

transfusion Passing a liquid, often someone else's blood, into the bloodstream.

transplant An organ or piece of tissue put into a patient's body which has been taken from another living thing.

trepanning Cutting a hole in the skull. This was once done to free evil spirits, but is still carried out sometimes, for example to allow brain surgery to be carried out.

V

vaccination To inoculate or feed a person with a vaccine made up of weakened microbes, in order to create immunity from a disease.

virus A tiny, simple microbe. Viruses cause many common infections, such as flu and colds.

Hypocr.   Galenus   Auicen.

Galen's writings

Index